Selected Poems

Barbara Crooker

FUTURECYCLE PRESS
www.futurecycle.org

Library of Congress Control Number: 2014959376

Copyright © 2015 Barbara Crooker
All Rights Reserved

Published by FutureCycle Press
Lexington, Kentucky, USA

ISBN 978-1-938853-70-8

For Richard, encore et toujours

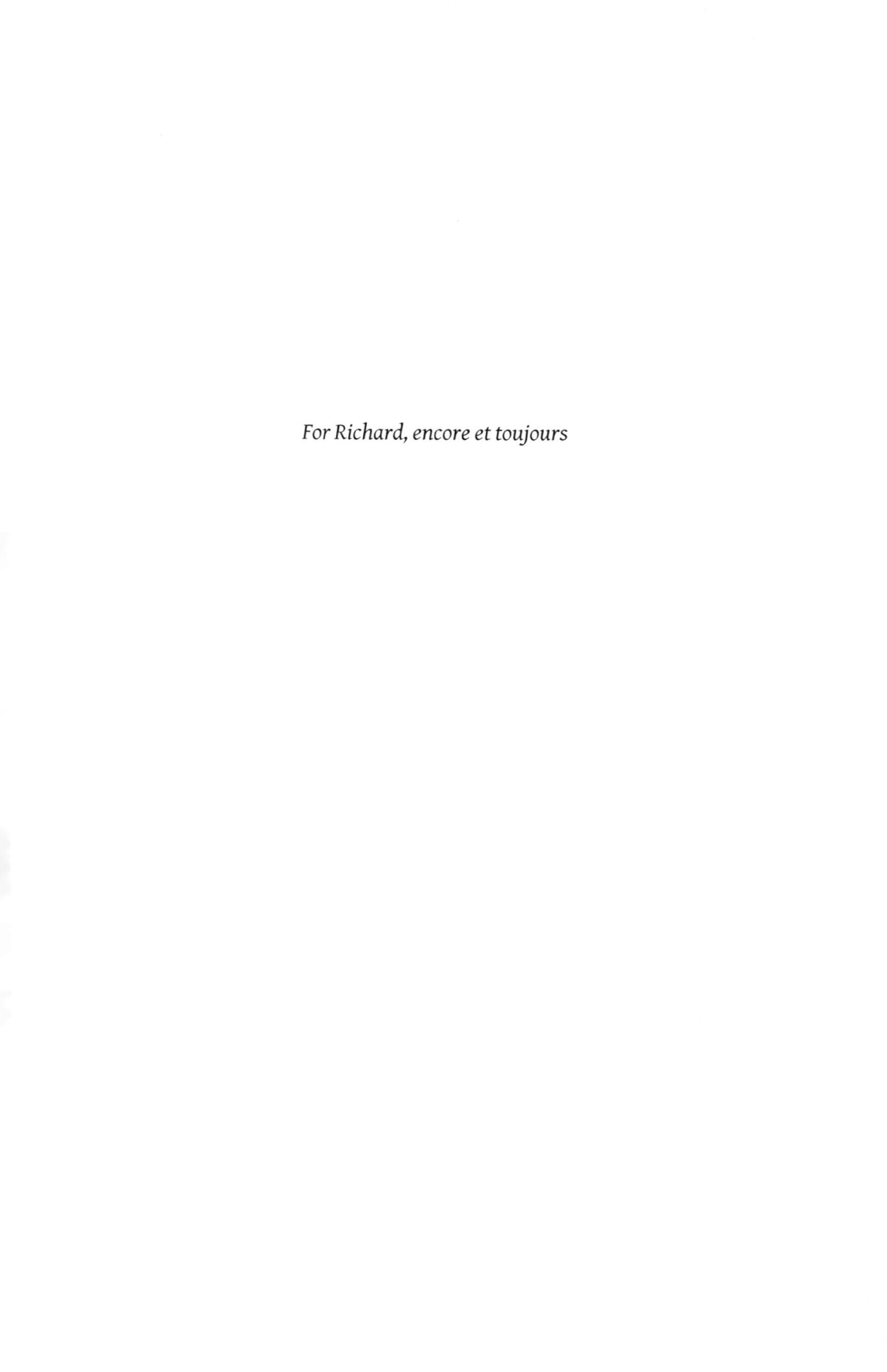

Contents

Foreword 9

from
ORDINARY LIFE

Ordinary Life 15
Doing Jigsaw Puzzles 16
Echolalia and the Mockingbird 17
Form & Void 18
The Shell Gatherers of Sanibel 19
The Stone 20
Throw a Stone in the Water, See the Ripples Spread 22
The Children of the Challenger League Enter Paradise 23
Personal Best 24
Driving Under the Clerestory of Leaves 26
Visiting the Pumpkin Farm 27
The Mother of a Handicapped Child Dreams of Respite .. 28
The Last Woman in America to Wash Diapers 29
Grating Parmesan 30
25th Reunion 32
Winter Light 33

from
WRITING HOME

Audubon Life List 37
Southern Tier 38
The Rose Villanelle 39
The Snow White Sestina 40
Auguries 42
Fever 43

from
STARTING FROM ZERO

10th Anniversary 47
January Thaw 49

from
LOOKING FOR THE COMET HALLEY

After the Storm 53
Looking for The Comet Halley 54
Rebekah Ziegler at the Quilting 56
Persistence 58

from
THE LOST CHILDREN

The Lost Children 63
Recipe for Grief 64

Burn Unit...65
Florida..66
Learning to Speak Neurosurgery...67
American Pastime..68
Raspberries..69
Field Guide to North American Birds...70
Diminuendo..71
A Month of Sundays..72
Christ Comes to Centralia...74
Skating After School..75

from
OBBLIGATO

Looking for Loons...79
Obbligato...80
Patty's Charcoal Drive-In..82
Unclaimed Salvage & Freight..84
Postcards from Hawaii...85
Gardening in a Dry Year..86
Amusement Park..87
The Wine Tasting..88
Summer Women...89
The Refugees...90
Paper Money..91
Coming in from the Cold...92

from
IN THE LATE SUMMER GARDEN

Rosa Multiflora...95
At the Château..96
Yes...98
Writers' Colony...99
My Friend E-Mails That She'd Like to Quit Her Job,
    but She Doesn't Have Time..100

from
PARIS

At the Cimitière de Montmartre..103

from
IMPRESSIONISM

At the Atelier Cézanne..107

from
THE WHITE POEMS

Prologue: Meditations on Grass..111
Because the Body Is a Flower...112

1992: Faith...113
October Light...114
Meditation in Mid-October...115
November, Sky Full of Bruises,..116
Total Eclipse of the Moon..117
1993: Hope...118
For a Friend Lying in Intensive Care Waiting for Her White
    Blood Cells to Rejuvenate After a Bone Marrow Transplant.......119
And Then, The Mastectomy...120
Breasts..121
Losing a Breast...122
Equinox...123
1994: Mercy...124
Dogwoods, Virginia..125
In the Late Summer Garden..126
She Tells the Dealer, Three More Cards.....................................127
1995: And She Never Gave Up,...128
Requiem..129
Letter to Judy..130

UNCOLLECTED POEMS

The Year Winter Never Came..133
Leaving the White In..134
Shoveling at Night..135
Making Strufoli...136
Worlds End..137
In January, My Middle Daughter Leaves Home..........................138
Snow Geese...139
Bright Star...140
Sadness Falls...141
Sorrow Puts on Her Blue Dress..142
Nine Days in April...143
Rapture...146
April Slips on Her Green Silk Dress,...147
Blue and White and Blue..148
August..149
Retriever...150
After September 11..151
Saying Good-Bye...152
Apples Fireworks Guns Ammo Honey Jelly................................153
All Souls' Day..154
Sewing..155
The Mothers..156

Foreword

Barbara Crooker's poetry is delicious and sad. Her world is lovely and finite. The two strains balance against each other—the beauty and joy of nature and love against the brutality and finality of loss. Finally I think what remains mostly with the reader is the beauty. The shimmer of life itself seems to be the strongest force of all. Life is not only individual, but is a force that connects. In "Equinox," a poem of about her friend's short remission during the course of her cancer treatment, she gives a brief poetics as well:

> she's come through it all, annealed by fire,
> calm settled in her bones like the morning mist in valleys
> and low places, and her hair's returned, glossy
> as a horse chestnut kept in a shirt pocket.
> Today a red fox ran through the corn stubble;
> he vanished like smoke. I want to praise things
> that cannot last.

How is it that Barbara Crooker's poems seem to console, even when they speak of grief? They are enhanced by a quirky metaphysics, not a religion in any kind of labeled can, but a sort of belief-without-borders that is rooted in a deep appreciation of the world and the intensity of love that knowledge of mortality provides. Her subject is ordinary life, including personal losses, the experience of raising an autistic child, travel and love. It is ordinary life but an extraordinary sensibility is experiencing it—leading the reader to realize that all life is exceptional, every experience meaningful.

These poems use startlingly original associations to develop their counterpoint. Her work is full of lush food images, which illustrate the verve of life while reminding us that these delights too are transient. Nature is a major presence throughout the work, and she has commented on her use of this imagery in an interview. To the question, "Any comments on your involvement with nature?" she responded:

> Frank Lloyd Wright said, "I believe in God, only I spell it Nature," and it seems to me that the closer we are to the natural world, the closer we are to our true spiritual selves. If I could write one line like Dylan Thomas's "The force that through the green fuse drives the flower," I could die happy. "The green fuse," for the animus of nature. Wow. Wallace Stevens said "One of the functions of poetry is that it gives you

a keener sense of being alive," and that's one of the things I'm after, being more connected, being more alive in this one life, the one that we're sleepwalking through....

That is the major function of Crooker's work—awakening. There are few such precise observers of the natural world, and fewer still who can so intuitively connect inner and outer weather. Colors, shapes, sounds, tastes, textures intensify and gleam. There is also a generosity to her vision—throughout her work we receive a constant sense of sharing, a natural sympathy with family, friends, even strangers. The details of her community make us more aware of our own. Her community is open and electric, lines of energy crackling along the bonds, reaching out to those beyond it, pulling them in.

The poems in this collection come mostly from chapbooks, collections which cluster around a theme, such as loss of a parent or friend, raising a child with autism, travel, art. Crooker's collections, both book-length and chapbook-length, are remarkable for their unity; their poems, epigraphs, even covers have a thematic thrust that collects and directs the work, making each a coherent work of art. What is surprising is that the Selected Poems should have this unity also, despite the fact that the contents are chosen from different chapbooks and uncollected work. Reading the work from beginning to end provides an experience of Crooker's world, that place of work and sadness balanced by art and love. It also provides vignettes of growing up in the fifties and sixties and shows what it was like to come of age as a woman in those years—the expectations, the hopes, the barriers that had to be overcome.

The stylistic devices are constant throughout the work—pileups of images that are almost violently sensual. Sentient fruits and vegetables speak to their consumers or observers. Synaesthesia is complex and strikingly astute. Repetition, run-on lines, rising and falling rhythms, and occasionally even rhyme control flow of verse and make it musical. Action verbs with the run-on lines electrify the work, giving it a high energy level. Even in poems of loss, the energy persists, giving us the sense that Crooker is truly in the current of life, feeling its verve—what Wallace Stevens called "the intensity of love" that he identified with "the verve of earth."

***

The poems at the very end of the collection have not appeared in the chapbooks but were published individually in journals. Perhaps these poems have a slightly different coloration from the rest—they are quieter, a little more autumnal. We see an older woman looking back over the road traveled, finding ironies, satisfactions, and sadnesses, and wondering at the richness of what is left. The images and connections in earlier works jump on one another's back, pile up, crackle. The connections in these poems are more meditative, quieter. There is energy even in her reflections. Readers who meet Barbara Crooker in this collection will want to get to know her further in her other four books.

—Janet McCann

Janet McCann is Professor of English at Texas A&M University, where she has taught since 1969. A 1989 NEA Creative Writing Poetry Fellowship winner, she has had poems in a variety of literary and popular journals. Her most recent poetry collection is *The Crone at the Cathedral* (Lamar University Press, 2013).

from
ORDINARY LIFE

Winner of the Byline Chapbook Prize, Byline Press, 2001

Ordinary Life

This was a day when nothing happened,
the children went off to school
remembering their books, lunches, gloves.
All morning, the baby and I built block stacks
in the squares of light on the floor.
And lunch blended into naptime,
I cleaned out kitchen cupboards,
one of those jobs that never gets done,
then sat in a circle of sunlight
and drank ginger tea,
watched the birds at the feeder
jostle over lunch's little scraps.
A pheasant strutted from the hedgerow,
preened and flashed his jeweled head.
Now a chicken roasts in the pan,
and the children return,
the murmur of their stories dappling the air.
I peel carrots and potatoes without paring my thumb.
We listen together for your wheels on the drive.
Grace before bread.
And at the table, actual conversation,
no bickering or pokes.
And then, the drift into homework.
The baby goes to his cars, drives them
along the sofa's ridges and hills.
Leaning by the counter, we steal a long slow kiss,
tasting of coffee and cream.
The chicken's diminished to skin and skeleton,
the moon to a comma, a sliver of white,
but this has been a day of grace
in the dead of winter,
the hard cold knuckle of the year,
a day that unwrapped itself
like an unexpected gift,
and the stars turn on,
order themselves
into the winter night.

Doing Jigsaw Puzzles

for David, age 4, who has autism

In "The Snow Queen," by Hans Christian Andersen, Kay, who has a splinter of glass from a hobgoblin's shivered mirror in his eye and heart, must solve a puzzle in order to win his freedom.

My son David is working his puzzles,
not wooden templates where the pieces
click neatly in their slots,
but ones of his own devising,
shapes moved to fit some other pattern.
If even a millimeter of space is off,
he throws the blocks from the table.
And Kay, in the Snow Queen's crystal palace,
works his pieces, trying to solve
the ice puzzles of reason,
must make the letters spell ETERNITY
to gain his freedom and a new pair of silver skates.
He doesn't succeed. But he goes on
and on, matching the borders
with his sharp flat pieces of ice,
fitting curve to curve,
straight line to straight line.
A silver splinter of ice
has lodged in his heart;
his blue fingers keep working the puzzle.
Soon, Gerda is coming, lips red as summer's roses.
She will thaw his hands; her tears will wash
the splinter out.

But David still sits here, working his blocks.
His eyes glaze over, his gaze is far away.
An invisible icy membrane
is cast over him like a caul.
Nothing in the world can touch his heart.
And love's first kiss won't break this spell.

Echolalia and the Mockingbird

The echo of the mockingbird resounds in our chimney
as he practices his warm-up scales—
a few high trills, a couple of cat calls—then
into his repertoire of cardinal, oriole, thrush,
repeated motifs, his own theme and variations.
Sound fills the yard, swirls into the trumpets of the lilies.
And my son David sings his own song:
snips of commercials, fragments of Sesame Street,
finger plays from school—echolalia, the speech
therapists call it, this repetition of what's heard,
sounds rebounding inside his head.
Last week in the supermarket,
he recited a month-old dialogue
between a friend and their teacher,
like an old television show that has
bounced into space or a late night
radio band from Kentucky, loud and clear.
In my ears, these snatches of both their melodies
reverberate, resound. And all I can do
is write it down, write it down.

Form & Void

For him [the autistic child], everything is form. —Jane Kessler

Glory be to God for dappled things...
All things counter, original, spare, strange.... —Gerard Manley Hopkins

The boy is blowing bubbles
with his mother, shimmering orbs
that glitter and dance
on the face of the lawn.
He prances after them, staring
with the deep mirror of his eyes
as they pop and disappear.
Flapping his arms, he chases them
toward the garden cosmos,
their mauve and lilac gowns
of silk voile waltzing
in the breeze.
He orbits around his mother
as she dips in her wand,
produces these baubles
from breath and film.
The glassy bubbles rise in a swirl
of pink and blue, a moment's iridescence.
This is the only magic the mother can conjure;
she cannot help him talk or say his name.
But they can do this together,
blow bubbles on a breezy afternoon,
make a strand of hand-blown beads
to grace the throat of the lawn.

The Shell Gatherers of Sanibel

stoop in the violet water,
sift through sand and broken fragments
for the fabulous, the rare: one perfect Junonia,
unmarred by the waves, or a Glory-of-the-Atlantic,
whorled and whole.
They have found translucent Lucinas,
angel wings, moon shells, butterflies;
still they keep searching.
The sky, the clouds, the sea—
heliotrope, mauve, mother of pearl—
the colors of coquina shells,
wings meeting like the wingbones
of a child's back.
This child, with hair so red it burns
the opal sky, is growing out of childhood.
Her mother wants to stop this sea change,
preserve her in amber,
let her only sorrow be
broken sand dollars, whelks, conches,
even as she knows time will move on,
will wash in like the waves,
will wash up starfish and rockweed
with equal indifference.
They sift through the sand again,
find lettered olives, alphabet cones.
No language that can hold this day.
Only the lavender sky.
Only the amethyst sea.

The Stone

was heavy.
The family carried it
with them, all day.
Not one
could bear
its weight, alone.
Yet how they loved it.
No other stone had
its denseness,
its particular way
of bending the light.
They could not take
the stone
out in public,
had to keep it home,
let it sing songs
in its own strange language,
syllables of schist and shale.
When the mother's back ached,
the father took the stone
for a while, then passed it
from sister to sister.
The stone
became a part of them,
a bit of granite
in the spine,
a shard of calcite
in the heart.
Sometimes
its weight
pressed them
thin, transparent
as wildflowers
left in the dictionary.

Sometimes
it was
lighter
than air.
The stone
did not talk.
But it shone.

Throw a Stone in the Water, See the Ripples Spread

We set up our tent, secure the gear,
and sink into the deep green quiet
of the woods, even though it's a state campground,
and boom boxes crackle by the campfires,
even though we've brought our children,
one of whom doesn't understand the meaning of silence,
but babbles in his own language like clear water
running in a stream or the lake water rippling
off the prow of our canoe as we drift at twilight;
the full moon spills its light in the water,
bullfrogs chug-a-rum in the cattails,
the thin blue smoke of campfires rises in the hemlocks,
circles the lake, a tart blue, the berries we picked
on the island where the bushes grew over our heads,
but now the dark tent of night covers the sky
and we drift off to sleep, soughed by the pines;
our breath in the tent rises, joins the small music
of the crickets and katydids, floats all the way
to the harmony of the stars.

The Children of the Challenger League Enter Paradise

The Challenger League is the handicapped division of Little League USA

Here in Little League heaven,
there will be no strikes against you
before you're up at bat,
no standards and regulations
to struggle against, no segregation,
no special education.
All the empty wheelchairs, braces, walkers.
No seat belts, head supports, drool bibs.
The crooked, straight. The rough places, plains.
No toy bats, wobbly tees, wiffle balls,
everybody-scores-outs-don't-count-rules.
These are the Major Leagues, stadium packed,
bases loaded, and the lights are on in the firmament.
Samantha winds up to pitch. David hits
a hard line drive deep to center. Adam
throws to Trevor, straight and true.
But here comes Jodie, stealing second,
then third, no longer held aloft by her dad,
while her legs windmill in the dust, no,
she's faster than the ink on a new contract,
she's sliding into home,
her smile bright enough
to power Detroit.

Personal Best

High summer, most of the flowers
done blooming, spent, intent on forming
seedpods, despite my relentless dead-
heading. Gone are the bachelor's buttons,
carnations, poppies, delphiniums, irises.
So we admire what's left: the rose of Sharon,
the day lilies, lemon yellow, fragrant and fresh,
doing their best to outshine
the sun by day, the moon by night.
And the mockingbird in the apple tree
is doing his best, most elaborate
summer song, a composition
of chickadee, cardinal, and rusty hinge.
The hot wind has dried the grass to wisps,
not lawn anymore but hay. The asters
and chrysanthemums slowly show their buds,
keep them tight, not yet, not yet.
The white glare of the sun is everywhere,
inescapable. When we drive under
an archway of trees,
we breathe in the shade like water,
the dappled asphalt a reef of coral fans,
green waves undulating over our heads.
Then we drive back into the spotlight,
the great white eye that reveals
our flesh softening with the years,
that has seared spots of cancer
on two friends this summer.

And cancer spreading unnoticed, like the grass
that will flourish unwanted in beds and borders
when the rains return, has sprouted again and again.
This flesh, ripening like mushrooms
in the compost of the woods.
And my son David picks mushrooms,
says *umbrella* and *it's raining, it's pouring*

even though it's the sun beating down,
drops of sweat beading on our arms.
Autism, I read recently, *is worse
than finding out your child has leukemia.*
And we go on, throwing him balls
he will never catch, buying him books
he'll never read, listening to his
speech, a mixed babble of commercials,
nursery rhymes, bits of conversation,
pushing him higher, higher on the swing,
into this high summer sky,
this tent of blue silk,
running with him around
the annual poppies
doing their best to color the border
with Mexican finery, their crêpe
paper skirts of fuchsia, magenta,
carnelian, gaudy piñatas.
Like weekend athletes running a 10K race
knowing they have no chance to win,
just hoping for a personal best,
we go on into this high summer,
the limitless sky cloudless,
the entire vegetable world running to fruit.

Driving Under the Clerestory of Leaves

We drive to your special education preschool
under an arch of maples, half green, half turned to gold,
the dark branches bold as the ribs
of a great cathedral, flying buttresses
that bend the light.
You haven't changed in the last two years,
developmentally delayed, mildly retarded,
school a struggle to stay in your seat,
say the beginnings of words,
point to colors and shapes.
While you wrestle with scissors,
daub with paste, I sit in the hallway,
trying to write, turn straw into gold.

When our two hours are spent,
we drive back up the hill toward home,
see the stand of mixed hardwoods
in full conflagration: red-gold, burnt orange,
blazing against the cobalt sky.
The architect who made these trees
was sleeping when he made this boy.
And my heart, like the leaves, burns and burns.

Visiting the Pumpkin Farm

The retarded children visit the pumpkin farm,
ride on a haywagon out to the fields
past acres of corn shocks dried and rustling,
the pale flax of a young girl's hair,
ready for silage, money in the till;
past stretches of dried weeds: foxtails,
chicory, goldenrod, good for absolutely nothing,
but, set against the late October sky
of darkened pewter, their golden seed heads
shining, beautiful unto themselves.

The Mother of a Handicapped Child Dreams of Respite

I want to drive away from all of this,
go clear to California, buzz out on the freeway
in a white Toyota, put on mirrored sunglasses,
cut off my hair, feel the hot desert air
on my bare arms, see a different moon, starker,
floating in the huge blue ether.
I will stop when I want to, visit a friend from college,
drink green tea by a koi pond under wisteria,
talk until our throats hurt about our complicated lives,
shopping in thrift shops, Thai cooking, about
how fucked-up men are, the many pathways to God.
I will sleep for an entire night, unbroken,
wake in light the color of chablis,
see Anna's hummingbirds at the nectar feeder,
eat granola and peaches for breakfast, eat avocados,
fresh figs, eat this entire edible state of California.
I will shower without having to arrange for child care,
let the steady ache between my shoulders melt away,
I will fall in love with my almond shampoo.
I will learn transcendental meditation,
spend a whole morning in a gallery,
hike in Yosemite where we watch Stellar's jays
in the piñons, surprise a coyote crunching bones.
Then, instead of dinner, I will eat ice cream.
I will dance until dawn in the jimsonweed,
I will dance in satin slippers at my broken boy's wedding,
I will drive clear to the Pacific and never come back.

The Last Woman in America to Wash Diapers

lugs the full pail down to the first floor,
heaves it in the washer, makes it spin its offal load.
How many diapers has she sloshed in the toilet,
how many neatly folded stacks has she raised skyward,
soft white squares of cotton, pieces of cloud,
how many double and triple folds has she pinned
on little bottoms? How many nights
of checking beds did she find those buns
raised in the air, loaves resting on a bakery shelf?
She knows the power of bleach, the benefits of rinsing.
On winter nights, when the snow comes down
in glittery drifts, she sees Ivory Flakes,
their slippery iridescence. When it comes
to dealing with the shit in her life,
nothing else is so simple, so white, so clean.

Grating Parmesan

A winter evening,
sky, the color of cobalt,
the night coming down like the lid on a pot.
On the stove, the ghosts of summer simmer:
tomatoes, garlic, basil, oregano.
Steam from the kettle rises,
wreathes the windows.
You come running when I reach for the grater,
"Help me?" you ask, reversing the pronouns,
part of your mind's disordered scramble.
Together, we hold the rind of the cheese,
scrape our knuckles on the metal teeth.
A fresh pungency enters the room.
You put your fingers in the fallen crumbs:
"Snow," you proudly exclaim, and look at me.
Three years old, nearly mute,
but the master of metaphor.
Most of the time, we speak without words.

Outside, the icy stones in the sky
glitter in their random order.
It's a night so cold, the very air freezes flesh,
a knife in the lungs, wind rushing
over the coil of the planet
straight from Siberia,
a high howl from the wolves of the steppes.
As we grate and grate, the drift rises higher.
When the family gathers together,
puts pasta in their bowls,
ladles on the simmered sauce,
you will bless each one
with a wave of your spoon:
Snowflakes falling
all around.

You're the weatherman
of the kitchen table.
And, light as feathers,
the parmesan sprinkles down,
its newly fallen snow
gracing each plate.

25th Reunion

A quarter of a century
since we left high school,
and we've gathered at a posh restaurant.
A little heavier, a little grayer,
we look for the yearbook pictures
caught inside these bodies of strangers.
Some of our faces are etched with lines,
the faint tracing of a lover's touch,
and some of our hair is silver-white,
a breath of frost. And some of us are gone.
But he's here, the dark angel,
everyone's last lover, up at the microphone
singing *Save the last dance for me;*
he's singing a cappella, the notes rising
sweetly, yearningly toward the ceiling,
which is now festooned with tissue flowers,
paper streamers, balloons.
And we're all eighteen again,
lines and wrinkles erased, gray hairs gone,
our slim bodies back, the perfect editing.
A saxophone keens its reedy insistence;
scents of gardenias and tea roses float in the air
from our wrist corsages and boutonnieres.
No children or lovers have broken our hearts,
it's just all of us, together,
in our fresh young skin,
ready to do it all over again.

Winter Light

It's a milkiness poured from
a great glass bottle,
a carafe of blanc de blanc, iced,
a light shot with pale gold,
opalescent blue,
the distillation of pearl....
In this icy light, the ghostly fronds
of ice ferns cover the glass
as the sky descends,
erasing first the far blue hills,
the cornfield hatchmarked with stubble,
coming to our street—
the sky flinging itself
down to the ground.
And the earth, like a feather bed,
accumulates layer on layer....
The snow bees are released from their hive,
jive and jitter, sting at the blinds.
Down here, under this glazed china cup,
the minor fracas of our little lives
is still under the falling flakes.
And the great abalone shell of the sky
contains us, bits of muscle, tiny mollusks.
These winter nights
are never black and dense,
but white, starlight
dancing off the land.
And then the luminous dawns,
the pearled skies full of hope
no matter what else we know.

from
WRITING HOME

Gehry Press, 1983

Audubon Life List

Last fall, birding on Hawk Mountain,
we perched for hours on the rocks
to watch the kestrels
wing in the thermals,
count kettles of broadwings
on calico hills.
We checked off accipiters,
buteos, raptors.
The touch of your hand
was like feathers.

Now you're gone,
the heart's in migration.
I drive north
on the four-lane
against all instincts,

and here, in the dying year,
I am left to measure
this loss, its insistence.
I am looking
for hawks
in the distance.

Southern Tier

I give you hardwood hills of orange and flame,
hardrock living in the hollows, where houses
are tar-paper tin-roofed cinder blocks, where the
shallow Chemung valleys the hillsides, and the
names are lost in their Indian past: Painted
Post, Big Flats, Horseheads, Elmira, Cohocton.
I give you finger lakes of glacial water,
long hard winters and brief sweet springs, where it is
overcast most of the year and the factory
smoke of Corning Glass Works clouds the crowned ridges,
the far hills to the north. Hilled in, houses flock
and crowd, nestled in hedgerows, braced for the snow.
Snow and flood are constants, but there are moments:
coined orange leaves, the gilded corn, jeweled crocus
braving the thin northern air. I give to you
Ithaca, Cayuga, Canandaigua, grape
vines, old schools, thin soil, rusty cars clumped in yards,
marigolds sunk in bathtubs, pinwheels in grass,
and always the hills, the gathering hills, and
the silver river ribboning the valley.

The Rose Villanelle

Everywhere I've lived I've planted roses
and though we've moved a lot, the roses stay.
Who knows what man disposes?

I've bled from thorny scratches on my toes.
One way or other, you pay.
Everywhere I've lived I've planted roses.

I dig the earth in awkward poses.
Planting for others makes me say—
I do not know how man disposes.

Peace, Proud Land, and Crimson Glory grow
in other yards. I do not get to stay
anywhere. I've lived; I've planted roses.

Sun-blind blue sky, the mocking crows
reflect the lack of heart I have today.
I do not know what that man proposes.

And I have shut my eyes; the rows
of green might just as well be gray.
Everywhere, I've lived. I've planted roses.
And man proposes, yes, and man disposes.

The Snow White Sestina

Snow White went walking in the wood
with her friend, the hunter, without care,
eager to find primroses, violets by the rocks.
She herself was dumb as stone, didn't see
the knife, feel a twinge in her coveted liver.
Her skin, snow; hair, ebony; lips, red as blood.

The hunter went back home, alone, the blood
of a boar on his weskit. The queen would
relish this dish: butter, mushrooms, heart and liver
of that wretched girl who taught her to care
about her fading looks: the lines, the silver, see-
ing nothing in her mirror but a wall of rock.

Now Snow White was alone in this wild and rocky
waste. Thorns scratched her legs, her stockings ran with blood.
The trees grew together and the sea
seemed very far away from this thick wood,
and as the branches beat her down, she ceased to care
about finding the way, about continuing to live.

But as you know, she did. Smelt bacon and liver
in the air, found a wee cottage made of rock
and timber. Had the strength to knock, left some blood
on the doorknob. Were the dwarves surprised? Did they care
if there was a woman in their house? Would
it make a difference? Wait and see.

Meanwhile, the queen, in her mirror magic, did see
Snow White and her chums carrying on. She lives!
She must die! And carrying ribbons, combs, and apples to that wood,
she set upon Snow White, whose head, you may recall, was full of rocks.
Twice the dwarves, finding her white, no blood
running, woke her up. But the apple stopped her cold, beyond caring.

The dwarves were washed with grief, laid her with care
on velvet pillows, cased with glass so they could see
her beauty: that clear skin, the night-dark hair, and even if no blood
flowed, to them it didn't matter anyway: alive
or dead, she was the same. They went away to split the rocks
with their picks; didn't see that prince come through the wood.

The lesson is: Stone up your heart. Don't care.
Life and blood are not as true as images.
Mirror the woods. Don't see. Don't see.

Auguries

This ground's a dead sea—
frozen mud, debris churned up
by winter frost heaves,
tractable as cement.
I prod and poke with an auger,
drill in the seed;
nothing can grow:
a season of zeroes,
a garden of stones.

But I will keep faith:
on the day of St. Patrick,
I will plant peas,
praying for green.
I will believe in June,
the return of the sun,
and I will taste the snap
of sugar
on my hungering tongue.

Fever

Geese stitch my sleep at night,
their cries thread my quilt-wrapped dreams;
the wind has changed.

Up on the hill, the farmer's turned
the cover of straw,
reversed the earth
to brown.

And here we are: blessed
in this first warm day of March:
snowdrops dotting piney ground,
aconites gold among stones.

We want to peel off layers
like sheets, run naked through
the greening grass.

Daffodil spears push
through dirt,
new growth shoots
from perennials,
and I look at you,
old love, the years roll back,
and my heart, that dumb bulb,
quickens, forced by the sun.
Heat and desire rise
from furrowed fields:
this is love you could burn for.

from
STARTING FROM ZERO

Great Elm Press and Foothills Publishing, 1987

10th Anniversary

Ten years ago, after the first night
we spent together,
we went to pick strawberries
knee-deep in furrows of scalloped leaves,
white flowers winking like stars.
It's still early morning,
but we're drunk on the winy air
and the headiness of our desire.
As we kissed more than we picked,
our mouths brushed like petals
rubbing in the wind,
our crimson fingers strayed
beyond the boundaries of clothing.
Stitch us in that tapestry forever,
baskets full of berries, and always in love....
But we had to go home,
turn the fresh fruit into preserves:
hull and cull the berries, crush them
with lemon, boil until thick
and sweet with yearning and sun.
Sealed in wax, each jar's stained glass,
full of the light.
And when we spread this redness
on morning toast, sparks
rekindle and glow.

And now it's ten years later.
Strawberry picking's an annual
task I do alone, or with a friend.
I boil the jam down to the clatter
of children underfoot.
And our eyes meet over curly heads
and our hands brush like green leaves in the wind....
And the jam shines in its cathedral of wax,
the sweetness of early June
poured in glass jars.

On January mornings,
when love and light are memories,
these red suns
light our cellar shelf.

January Thaw

False spring.
The sun, thinned
to a white radiance,
warms the bones,
pulses the thermometer up over sixty.
Crocuses push their tips
through the newly softened earth.
Too soon, we say,
and want to make them
retrieve their leaves,
refurl them back.
Shrink, before the snow returns,
or you won't live to dazzle us
with your watered silks
of purple, white, gold.
We haven't had a proper winter yet,
the ground still brown,
no real accumulations.
But in this fickle weather,
we warm, too,
turn our faces upward
to the light,
shed our coats, gloves, scarves.
Sheets of ice begin to fall away.
And suddenly, our skin is alive again.
Shyly, small flowers open in our hearts.

from
LOOKING FOR THE COMET HALLEY

Dawn Valley Press, 1987

After the Storm

passes, the wind rinses the sky to aquamarine.
In this clean new light, the corn is polished,
carved of jade, leaves of beryl, viridian;
the gold of the wheat fields, stripes of beaten ore.
Under this great glass eye
we stand, on the rim of summer,
the bones of winter under our feet,
washed again in this bright loud light.

Looking for The Comet Halley

> *What's the point of this comet anyway if you don't know when you've seen it?* —Becky Crooker, age 7

I
All day long, the wind has etched
an icy scrimshaw on the glass;
riding this northeaster,
the house creaks and sways.
At 10° and falling, we go out
into a world so cold, it could be
the last place on earth, Antarctica.
Our boots chink on the frozen lawn;
the backyard is transformed
in this mid-winter night.
On a summer day, our eyes are drawn
to islands of flowers shimmering in light,
but now the frozen lily beds
are hard as a cold kiln;
even the mulch has turned to rock.
The perennial gardens are shadowy patches,
bushes, hazards lurking in the dark.
Our eyes are drawn nowhere but up
to the taffeta canopy, starlight leaking
through warp and woof.
We're at the other end of the scope,
reduced, two small specks under an onyx dome.

II
We are not just mother and child,
but two star searchers voyaging through this night.
Light from suns long dead shines on us,
black holes swallow and yawn.
We read the star charts, parkas billowing,
the ship of the world careering in the vast black sea.
Up in the canopy, with no dotted lines,
the patterns are lost to us,
constellations unreadable.

But we manage to find Jupiter, clear and steady
in the southwest sky,
sight a fist at arm's length up,
then one star to the left,
and we think that we see Halley.
This comet does not come in glory,
trailing a tail as long as the Dipper,
making us gasp and point.
Instead, it's a frosty smudge in the glass,
a dirty snowball, the thumbprint of God—
And though we're disappointed
by our own expectations, the media razzle,
we're taken in by the blaze and glitter.
We turn in the dark and sail toward home,
the slanted yellow light reeling us in.
How vast this starry starry night,
how far and wide the ports between the stars.

Rebekah Ziegler at the Quilting

Today is a quilting.
I rise early, help Mama in the kitchen,
slice the bread, bring butter
up from the cellar where
it's always damp and cool.
I set places, spoon out jam.
The berries are still as red and sweet
as the June day we picked them.
The men will leave early today
in the gray morning light,
sun licking at fence rails,
the earth still and sleeping.
This will be a day for women,
the babies at our feet
playing under the tent
the batting makes;
Sarah and Rachel tending
the cooking, no stitchers they.
In and out, up and down,
our needles fly
fast as our tongues,
telling the news:
Sunshine and Shadows,
Crosses and Losses:
weddings, births, deaths,
and of those who stepped outside
the lines:
Drunkard's Path, Wild Goose Chase,
Rocky Road to Kansas,
Broken Dishes, Rolling Stone.
The earth gives, the earth grows quiet.
Idle hands the Devil's tool.
Corn waves to the horizon in summer,
snow blanks it out in winter.
Reuben sows the fields on the hill,
steals looks at me
under his black brim.

I will have made my twelfth quilt soon,
nine stitches per inch. The next
will be my marriage quilt.
I know from the English neighbors
that life can be different,
but I will live mine
in straight and narrow rows:
Double Wedding Ring, Garden Maze,
Ohio Rose, Morning Star,
The Tree of Life.

Persistence

for Karl Patten

After the heat of an August day,
as the earth cools off and the sweetness of cut grass rises,
I stop from the endless weeding to look around,
admire the delphiniums, fountains of blue,
cool notes in a yard of green, green, green,
and survey the damage from last night's foraging.
My enemy's not an army of slugs, tracks of silver
left on the battlefield,
or an invasion of locusts
whose monotonous artillery rings
through the long hot afternoons.
No, we're talking rabbit here,
I mean, *bunny,* the cliché of softness,
from its velveteen fur to the white surprise of tail,
for God's sakes, we're talking
Bugs, Peter, Flopsy, Mopsy, Benjamin....
Forgive me, Beatrix, but as night hops in
on its padded feet, everything growing goes under.
The lilies are under siege, savaged by those tiny teeth,
effective as shears. The Asiatics' red flames are doused,
the pink and gold Aurelian trumpets silent,
and the Orientals' recurved blooms,
all gone with a nip of the whiskers.
And in the vegetable patch: disaster.
The broccoli plants, once three feet wide,
cool jade leaves wide as sails
crowned with clusters of florets
are now a radiant of ribs, pale green bones,
nibbled to the nub.
What was parsley is a bouquet of stems,
the carrots are topless, woe to the parsnips.
I try a witches' brew of remedies:
dried blood, mothballs, hot pepper,
seasonings for the lapin salad, additional zest and nip.
Now they're asking for croutons.

Another writer tells me he read in a poem
how the speaker pisses on the ground,
marking his territory,
drawing the boundaries with a golden stream.
So my husband and I fill night jars,
tumblers of amber, as much volume
as we can muster, and I incant
as I pour, be gone, be gone.

For a time, it works,
but steady rains destroy our progress.
And the bunnies creep back, peer towards the house.
As the rain pours down, they nestle under
the swing set, get out the good china, pour tea.
Hello, they say, hello, old friends, we're home.

Barbara Crooker | 59

from
THE LOST CHILDREN

The Heyeck Press, 1989

The Lost Children

The ones we never speak of—
miscarried, unborn,
removed by decree,
taken too soon, crossed over.
They slip red mittens in our hands,
smell of warm wet wool,
are always out of sight.
We glimpse them on escalators,
over the shoulders of dark-haired women;
they return to us in dreams.
We hold them, as they evanesce;
we never speak their names.
How many children do you have?
Two, we answer, thinking three,
or three, thinking four;
they are always with us.
The lost children come to us
at night and whisper
in the shells of our ears.
They are waving goodbye
on schoolbuses,
they are separated from us
in stadiums,
they are lost in shopping malls
with their fountains and pools,
they disappear on beaches,
they shine at night in the stars.

Recipe for Grief

My grandmother is dying in the hospital.
I cannot comprehend these words,
cannot feel grief, not yet.
Instead, I slice eggplant in a sunny kitchen,
dust it, pat each slice gently.
The flour is as fine and white as her skin.
I enter the ritual:
from flour to eggs to crumbs to oil,
moving in a pattern old as Corsica.
Working against burns and spills,
I assemble the golden slices,
alike as a party of aunts,
tomato sauce fragrant
with basil, oregano,
creamy mozzarella,
pungent parmesan.
In the heat of the oven,
they will meld
into something unlike the sum of their parts.
I've heard her voice in every direction,
her hands are working in mine,
as we create sun-drenched Italy, ancient hills of thyme.
Fragrance steams from the oven as the heady flavors mingle:
this parmigiana, this sacrament, this easing of the heart.

Burn Unit

A cup of coffee,
usual as morning,
who'd have seen it as danger,
the knife's edge, the ungated stairs?
But there it was,
the baby's hand quicker than the eye,
and the black liquid searing his skin,
peeling it back like a translucent onion.
He screams, and we, his protectors, are frozen.
Even ice won't quench this fire.
The rest of the day, a blur—
emergency rooms, hospital procedures,
and then we have him back,
the damaged arm waving like a badge
in its gauze cocoon.
My little hero, it's only me you have
to save you from what's waiting in the dark:
the lovely red poinsettia,
the friendly setter without his shots,
Drano's shining crystals,
pieces of hot dogs, hard candies,
such a black litany....
Oh, I buckle you in for each ride,
trickle vitamin drops down your throat,
steam carrot coins into orange slush,
but underneath that putty-soft skin,
how quickly the bruise blooms,
the windpipe closes....
I want to swaddle you in bulletproof clothes,
lie down in front of traffic,
anything, to keep
that red tree inside your skin
branching, growing.

Florida

Going south
for the first time
to the land of salt
and sand, palm trees, hibiscus.
Back home,
it's winter, the garden hard
and cold as an ironworks,
but here, flowers in shades of sherbet,
green trees lit up by oranges
glowing round as gaslights.
Pelicans swoop down beside us,
squadrons of B-52 bombers
from 1940s movies.
Silver moss hangs from trees,
drifts of old lace curtains.
We lie on the deck,
our pale northern skin
drinking the sun.
Our bones are turning to coral.
We lie like reefs
jeweled by brightly colored fishes,
work and schedules forgotten,
snowed in the north forever,
and we who have travelled
so far in time
turn to gold in the sun.

Learning to Speak Neurosurgery

An April afternoon of pale green light,
dogwood dappling the lawn.
The heart, that stingy fist, begins to open,
generous as apple blossoms
to the fumbling bees.
I watch the baby crawl on the new grass,
bewildered as a foal
at this strange green carpet.
His head is still so soft it pulses.
In the coral of his brain,
CAT scans reveal a gray fish
swimming an inland sea.
We've learned the names of unspeakable words:
brain damage, stroke, cancer.
The apple blossoms light up the tree,
stars in a green sky.
Fragrance lifts from his skin
the way the clouds of phlox loft
their scent at night.
Spring, with its rumor of new life,
has never seemed more false.
The white lilacs shimmer in the wind.

American Pastime

A June morning, the air hung with the scent of roses
as my mother irons, filling the kitchen with steam.
She sprinkles the laundry with water from a ketchup bottle,
showers the sheets, blesses the shirts.
Everything is pressed, even dishcloths.
Outside on the line, towels smell of wind.
The stack grows taller as the morning wanes.
Soon, there will be sandwiches,
tuna glistening with mayonnaise
on crushable white bread,
drinks made from syrup in lurid colors.
And then the long, long afternoons,
the sun, pitched and searing as a hardball
coming at you fast and clean.
Swinging hard, you connect,
hickory to rawhide,
a moment hanging in time,
stretching fresh and clean as the sheeted sky,
when days were caught, suspended,
when the dark meant only hide and seek
or time to come home.

Raspberries

Fall crop:
juicy drupelets,
carmine thimbles,
little beehives, ruddy nipples
dangle from the arching branches,
fall lightly into our cupped hands.
Just a touch uncouples
these plump droplets
from their cores.
The centers are hollow;
our tongues just fit.
Crushed in our mouths,
the berries turn to wine;
even the bees
are drunk on this redness.
O September!
When the rest of the garden
dwindles to meager,
when the trees begin
their strip to the bones,
you come to fruit
bearing rubies on your canes,
and we're on our knees,
stained in crimson,
our garnet fingers
praising the earth.

Field Guide to North American Birds

The watchers wade and wait in the water,
half hidden in rushes and cattails,
binoculars aimed at the sky
which is, for the untrained,
a lidless blue, blank and unoccupied.

Bird at 1 o'clock,
they cry, as a mote appears,
a speck of brown.
Could it be a crested dowager?
    an olivaceous private?
    a hooded academic?
No, no, it's a northern snitch—
    see the buff rump,
    the dark moustache,
    the spectacles.

We who have no field marks,
who lose the flight patterns
from our scopes,
stand dumb in the mud,
no checks on our life lists,
tone-deaf to the twitters around us,
the ethereal flutelike tones
of farthingale,
    martinet,
    quark.

Diminuendo

Late August, and the fields are singing with insects,
goldenrod blessing the air.
The hillside springs with grasshoppers
drunk on the last dregs of sun.
Queen Anne's lacework is edging the path
where even the grasses are shining silver,
lifted, as in common prayer,
by the diminishing wind.
Out in the fields, the corn stands shock still;
the stalks have become the color of air.
Their fingers point north, where the snow is waiting.
All of the apples have gathered in redness;
a thousand sunsets burn in the trees.
Soon, they will drop and split,
and the whirling wasps
will leave only the cores,
the spaces that remain.

A Month of Sundays

Waiting,
for church to be over,
restless,
in your starched dress,
stiff sash;
above you,
the steady current
of the sermon murmurs....
Then waiting,
for company to come,
the clock barely ticking,
your toes hard as pebbles
in the pinch of patent leather....
And when they finally come,
the white-curled ladies
with their flowered dresses,
scented with lavender and time,
how soon the rush of admiration
for how much you've grown,
how smart you've become,
passes by,
like a river parting
around a stone,
and the conversation bends
to grown-up talk.

And waiting, waiting,
for the proper Sunday dinner:
a roast crackling on the platter,
boats of gravy, endless vegetables,
a row of pies....
And then, the decline of the afternoon,
when it is always 4 o'clock,
no matter how many board games you play,
the colored wooden pieces
moving in the spaces....

Or how many scratchy 78s
you listen to on the hi-fi,
while the talk still swirls
above and around you,
the minutes lasting longer
than they ever will again.
And waiting, for the finally doled-out candy:
chocolates elegant in silver foil
and dark crenellated paper cups,
looking better than they taste,
so many choices:
nougats, caramels, cherries, creams.

Christ Comes to Centralia

in the late Appalachian autumn;
dark culm looms behind the town,
papery birches the only thing living.
Unemployed miners sit in bars,
their clapboard houses tight against the hill,
looking like blocks that might all fall down,
topple and tipple.
Women in babushkas and dark coats
shuffle down Centralia's streets
past boarded-up houses.
Wisps of smoke rise from the ground.
A young girl passes the abandoned school,
her eyes anthracite in a pasty face.
Think of this: Hell under Main Street!
Crevasses yawning in backyards
next to jungle gyms and swing sets,
steam venting by the onion-domed church,
blue light coming from its fractured windows.
And where is our Lord?
With the dispossessed,
their roots to this Pennsylvania coal town
deep and branching as the black veins that spread,
underriddled by fire pulsing as blood.

He is here on the skin of this earth,
in a Steeler's jacket and knit cap,
helping to pack the last cardboard box,
looking back before the bulldozers come.
Overhead, a crow spreads its glossy feathers,
a chunk of coal tossed in the colorless sky.

Skating After School

In the space between school and supper,
light flat as a china plate,
sky and ice a single seam
stitched by black trees,
we raced over the railroad tracks,
down an embankment to the frozen pond,
snow embroidering our flannel jeans.
Then out, onto the ice, blades dividing
the surface into geometry,
ice writing from an old language
until it's a blackboard in need of erasing.
And, as the baggage of school disappeared,
ephemeral as smoke from the bonfire
where we charred hot dogs, made dark cocoa
that burned our tongues,
we went back out onto the ice again,
feeling the slap and chock of the hockey puck,
the ache of air inside our lungs....
And as the dark came down like a coffee cup,
we saw the lights come on up over the tracks.
But we kept playing, icing the puck,
shooting straight for the goal,
legs aching beyond endurance....
Home, where the yellow lights were growing,
filled with the smell of macaroni and cheese
and muffins, but we stayed out, still checking and hitting
wood against wood, our steel blades marking the ice.
And, when we knew we could not stand it
any longer out in the cold,
we clambered up the banks,
falling on the cinders,
woodsmoke and winter clinging to our clothes,
climbing, climbing, toward the steady yellow lights of home.

from
OBBLIGATO

Linwood Publishers, 1991

Looking for Loons

This poem doesn't want to be written,
stalled like a stationary front, going nowhere,
elusive as a loon that's diving in dark water
and surfacing—where? We both guess
where it will rise, but we're never right.
At night, its call ripples in my sleep,
a trail of liquid Os dancing in the wake.

Like paddling our canoe in Penobscot Bay,
where it's lunacy to take a canoe out in the open water
at the mercy of the following tides,
drifting without destination; you, sitting stern,
wearing my favorite shirt the color of falling leaves,
your hands firm on the paddle
just as last night, in our nylon tent,
they knew how to stroke my body into love.
I look at your face, which is on fire,
and know that this exact feeling will not come again,
will fade the way a campfire eventually goes out,
sparks flying up to the dark pines.

But still we take our green canoe camping,
going nowhere, poking around the edges of a lake,
still looking for loons, who surface when we least
expect them, their round vowels rising
in the pine-dark night. I turn from the bow, we kiss,
and my knees turn to water. The way this poem,
in spite of itself, burns to be written,
surfaces like the ripples our paddles make
as they dip in the water, spreading in circles
and growing, a quiver of notes
in the throat of the pines.

Obbligato

The burble of house wrens colors the air.
It's early summer, and everything is possible.
The irises shine in their silken petals;
peonies have burst into cerise, magenta, cream.
The lawn is impossibly lush and green
to us, who know how soon August comes with its hot breath,
who see the grass dry and thin under this lavish verdure,
who know how the earth shuts down like an iron fist
and are still transfixed.
And what the house wren babbles,
the mockingbird repeats,
adding trills and cadences of its own,
embroidering in the liquid notes of thrushes,
the scree of the swing set, doing a riff on
the endless cheer! cheer! cheer! of the cardinal,
bird with no song of its own and everyone else's in its heart.
This heart's been tight as a peony bud
waiting for rain;
how briefly it blooms,
resplendent in its carmine longing.
What a hard carapace
old loves and losses have built up,
years of chitinous excretions,
but even it can break.

I used to want to hold onto friends for life,
mourned each falling off, each move away,
but now I see them drifting in and out of our lives,
careless and gorgeous as blossoms
wandering in the wind,
which blows, as we know, wherever it pleases.
But no matter how short, our lives have been blessed.

We live in a land without famine or war;
each night we smooth down into the grace of sheets.
How we forget to be grateful.

In the morning we will have fresh fruit,
and music and news.
Roses will scent the air.
And all that we have forgotten,
the mockingbird will repeat
into the small green spaces
of our still unripened hearts.

Patty's Charcoal Drive-In

First job. In tight black shorts
and a white bowling shirt, red lipstick
and bouncing ponytail, I present
each overflowing tray as if it were a banquet.
I'm sixteen and college-bound;
this job's temporary as the summer sun,
but right now it's the boundaries of my life.
After the first few nights of mixed orders
and missing cars, the work goes easily.
I take out the silver trays and hook them to the windows,
inhale the mingled smells of seared meat patties,
salty ketchup, rich sweet malteds.
The lure of grease drifts through the thick night air.
And it's always summer at Patty's Charcoal Drive-In—
carloads of blonde-and-tan girls
pull up next to red convertibles,
boys in black tee shirts and slick hair.
Everyone knows what they want.
And I wait on them, hoping for tips,
loose pieces of silver
flung carelessly as the stars.
Doo-wop music streams from the jukebox,
and each night repeats itself,
faithful as a steady date.
Towards 10 p.m., traffic dwindles.
We police the lot, pick up wrappers.
The dark pours down, sticky as Coke,
but the light from the kitchen
gleams like a beacon.
A breeze comes up, chasing papers
in the far corners of the darkened lot,
as if suddenly a cold wind had started to blow
straight at me from the future—
I read that in a Doris Lessing book—

but right now, purse fat with tips,
the moon sitting like a cheeseburger
on a flat black grill,
this is enough.
Your order please.

Unclaimed Salvage & Freight

> *will sacrifice one million dollars worth of furniture in their parking lot this Saturday. —radio announcement*

First, we have the ceremonial scattering of ashes
from marbleized ashtrays in animal forms.
Then, the victims compose themselves in groupings:
rec rooms, breakfast nooks, entertainment pits.
It is important to sacrifice a virgin:
only the purest naugahyde will do.
How can we feel guilt?
This hide-a-bed's been concealing its trysts,
and look at that Lazy Boy, plump and smug,
thinking it can recline behind the sectional
and miss our searching eyes.
Did you ever see such arrogance?
The armoire will not come forward,
thinks its veneer will save it from the fire.
As the pyre towers, sparks fly over the crowd
like love-crazed fireflies searching for mates.
The flames roar: more, more,
as wingbacked chairs are turned into kindling;
whole dining rooms of cherry and chintz,
Queen Anne tables with cabriole legs
add to the fire, raising it higher
into the night, lighting the faces in the crowd.
Men lick their lips, women twist strands of hair,
waiting. Lust rises like smoke.

Bring out the breakfronts!
Melt down those brass bedsteads!
Hump the camelback sofas!
Light, I say, more light, more light!

Postcards from Hawaii

The coconut palms are swaying in the Trade Winds—
Trade Winds—the very name echoes, sending up
clipper ships, cargoes of spice and silk....
One night, the moon was so bright you could read by it,
writing a path of silver on the restless Pacific,
shimmering, shimmering.
The next, the moon set early, the stars reigned,
ebbing and throbbing, the black silk night alive with fire.
What does this mean? What is the ocean murmuring
with its endless refrain, repeat, repeat?
Whatever is said is echoed by the palm fronds
as they clatter and rasp in the wind.
There is so much to write, in this spin of time,
but everything rattles on in its usual pace.
And these white pages with their black alphabets
have no more permanence than tracks in the sand.
Here, almost every tree is blooming:
the flame trees, the golden showers.
The air is sweet with plumaria,
and the fish are jewels:
ornate wrasse, Moorish idols, yellow tang.
Yet as I write this down, the present slips away,
receding like the coastline at Kapaa.
Surely there are people who travel, uncompelled to record the journey.
But the words flow on, sand drifting through fingers.
Each day we put on the hot blue sky like a headdress of flowers.
And at night, your skin is incandescent,
its own source of heat and light.
And none of this has an ending,
trails off like the long white tail of a tropicbird
circling over a green glade.
There is a waterfall by the left-hand side of the picture.
Everything is diffused in light.

Gardening in a Dry Year

The sky is a hard blue bowl,
unmarred by even a smear of cloud, a hint of rain.
No promises here.
The long-term forecast shrieks sun, sun, sun.
Seedlings shrivel,
cucumbers contract on the vines.
The loam, once dark and rich
as a chocolate torte,
crumbles to dust
that sifts in the desultory wind.
Gardening is the language of loss.
Enemies are legion:
cutworms, slugs, snails, caterpillars;
tomato hornworms, fat and green,
studded with wasp eggs;
rodents and rabbits, fungus and fireblight,
more than the ten plagues of Egypt.
What we love and water,
bless with the sprinkler's silver spray,
does not necessarily thrive.
We can fertilize and mulch,
double-dig and retrench,
but we're helpless as wheat
in a sudden summer storm,
our prayers of intercession dry dust in our mouths,
dumb as our glib tongues, the desert of our hearts.

Amusement Park

The air spins with the smell of sugar.
On the rides, the children whirl,
shrieks lacing the air, rising and falling.
The machines hum, almost alive,
and we trust them to return those bodies
intact. Where did we lose our faith?
When did we start to think
the ride might not be over?
That the Scrambler might
rearrange limbs on the concrete,
or the Tilt-a-Whirl permanently
alter our center of gravity?
When did Bumper Cars start to feel
too much like the turnpike
and the Ferris Wheel,
a parachute drop
from an airplane in flames?
The colored lights no longer look
like careless jewels
flung against a velvet sky.
We fear the child-snatcher
lurking behind the striped tent,
don't believe we'll win a unicorn
with a fistful of skeeball tickets.
We know what lurks in the tunnel of love
and that cotton candy isn't nibbling on a cloud.
But still, we take them here,
our children, our treasures,
holding their sticky hands,
lifting them onto the wooden horses,
cream-colored and licorice-black,
as they gallop on their mirrored track,
floating to the rise of the calliope's song,
and we even urge them on, saying
catch the brass ring, catch the brass ring.

The Wine Tasting

The connoisseurs meet to drink and compare,
roll redness on their tongues,
inhale the heady air,
rate and bicker.
Watch them make their lists:
there's a noble Lucent
and a crisp Charisma, estate-bottled.
Perhaps they'll include some old Patina
or a robust Lamborghini.
What about a Raddichio—
such a prominent nose!
Or sweet liqueurs—
a golden Mellifluous,
a delicate Gallinule.
Around the oaken library table
they sit and compare,
weigh and measure
the savor and bouquet
of such a chosen few:
a Roseola '68
an Annelid '80
or a Clairvoyant from any even year.

Summer Women

The warm May sun has brought them out,
these summer women—hair streaked with light,
limbs already turning golden.
They belong on the courts,
so graceful, so stately,
returning perfect backhands.
They never sweat.
Beside them, we seem less
(or more, if our flesh exceeds
the bounds of propriety, or shorts),
our imperfections magnified
in the dazzling light.
This is never-land, where messy life,
with its bills and children, does not intrude,
where happiness is attainable,
desires fulfilled,
and if it equals zero,
they'll call it love.

The Refugees

From my kitchen I see
large white birds sailing
in the distance,
a familiar crook of wing.
I grab my glasses in disbelief:
seagulls in March? And so far inland?
The wind washes like surf;
the corners of my mouth taste salt.

Later, I read in the paper
of this annual flight;
see a grainy print of an Amish farmer
warding off their wheeling wings—
"They'll steal my worms," he cries.

Later, I am at a table,
trying to teach English
to a family from Vietnam.
They have lived three years in camps;
they came with nothing but their names.
My letters are bird tracks in the sand;
their words fly back and forth between them,
bird songs on the tongue.

Oh, this long slow flight through language—
years before we will talk together.
Seagulls, this far inland,
seagulls in Pennsylvania—
working their wings for the long flight home.

Paper Money

for Denh Khai Voong, Quang Ninh, Vietnam

It is October:
maple trees rain gold
on the streets.
You have no money;
your father in Hong Kong writes:
eat less.
Each day the rice bowl shrinks.
When they come, when your parents come,
you will find work,
you will save your sick husband,
you will feed your babies.
Today the social workers
tore up November—
maybe December, maybe later.
"Wait"—I point to it in the dictionary.
"Soon, soon," I croon, an empty bowl of adverbs.
I am the friend
you cannot talk to:
we have so few words between us,
and only for things, like bread and air.

Outside, the chestnut leaves burn
copper and bronze.
What is Vietnamese for red tape?
If it translates to ribbon of red,
how will you know what I mean;
my hands are bound.
Someone in Hong Kong
is taking bribes, gold
coins or rings.
How can we pay?
Each day, your life dims.

Coming in from the Cold

after John Le Carré

We have used all our tradecraft
to erect barriers, create covers—
deep background.
We've recruited networks
to protect us: legmen,
lamplighters, watchers.
Our tools are fallbacks,
dead drops, letterboxes;
we speak in codes and ciphers.
Yes, we've travelled back alleys,
gone to the earth.

Now our safe houses are known,
our agents are on the run,
cover is blown skyhigh—
listen:
love is crossing the border.

from
IN THE LATE SUMMER GARDEN

H & H Press, 1998

Rosa Multiflora

What was a good idea gone bad, using wild roses as a living fence
to contain cattle. Now they ramble unchecked, grow in waste areas:
weeds, pests, nuisances. In June, thousands and thousands
of white blossoms light my back path. They spring up everywhere,
wander from the mulberries to honeysuckles, grow up the old apple trees,
cover the hillside with brambles and blooms. Imagine them covering
a castle, the nasty task the Prince had to snip and hack his way
to true love's heart. The hearts of these roses are golden,
tiny, covered with bees. Now June pulls us fully open,
awake, this sweet heavy air, petals under our feet, on the lawn.
This is the season of transformation, when something unasked
for can turn to love. Try to get these roses out by lopping
or pesticides, burn them with fire, level the ground.
They will multiply before your eyes, growing back stronger,
thicker, thornier. We could curse the ground, or we could praise
what is there: cups of honey and cream that spill in the air.

At the Château

> *Life struggles to copy that French château.*
> —Stephen Dobyns, Body Traffic

Where Madame brings you a cup of *café noir*,
rich and dark, and a simple *petit déjeuner*
of the best bread you ever tasted, thick golden crust,
sweet butter, *confiture* of wild strawberries, *les fraises des bois.*
Mornings here are busy blurs: alarms clang, the kettle screams,
homework is lost, clothes aren't ironed,
everyone hidden behind a wall of newsprint.
But at the château, you eat on a terrace overlooking the sea,
lavender and mimosa in the air. You feed your lover
pieces of croissant, remember last night, the linen sheets,
the lovely silk of skin. In this life, laundry streams,
ironing looms mountainous, the furniture shrugs
into its coat of fine gray dust. But through the open *porte,*
the château beckons in its marble perfection, every carved
molding and lintel painted in gold leaf, and oh! the damask
bedclothes! Oh! the mirrored hallways, the crystal chandeliers,
diamonds dripping from the ceilings, *ciel,* the word for heaven.
Fat cherubs and plump angels frolic in oil paintings,
caught forever in their gilt frames, and light is refracted
and refined from every faceted surface.
In this life, meals roll out like Os, like baby birds
opening their beaks screeching for more.
Where the finest meal you muster can't compete
with soft steamed burgers smeared with condiments
in their styrofoam nests, salty fried potatoes,
shakes of iced cement. Glancing out the drive-thru *fenêtre,*
you see china place settings, ivory candles,
a bowl of pink roses, crystal glasses of Puilly-Fuissé.
Un peu de pâté? Or *mousse au saumon?*
Then a light *salade* of spring greens sprinkled with violets.
A delicate white fish in a *beurre blanc.* A brisk *sorbet.*
A kaleidoscope of cheeses: hard, soft, goat's, sheep's,

ripened, fresh, spice-studded, herb-strewn. A dark cup
of espresso. And a *marquise au chocolat,* with raspberries
scattered around. For it's *l'heure bleu,* night waltzing
in with her blue satin gown, a dazzle of stars at her throat
and wrists. A violin concerto enters the kitchen,
its rich opulent tones like the perfume of beautiful women.

Yes

Today, the sun pours out like jam,
summer almost gone, and what comes
next. But here it is, the great yes,
the ain't it good to be alive yes,
the even though the last deadline's coming yes,
that final call for submissions yes,
and I'm sitting here with my yellow notebook,
letting the sun spill on my bare arms,
listening to the crickets' brassy song.
There's a touch of woodsmoke in the air,
a rumor of frost on the lawn, here, in buttery
October, and I'm writing as fast as I can.

Writers' Colony

Here, we are sequestered, cloistered, in our habits,
walking down a narrow path hedged in by boxwood,
walled off from the world. Heads bowed
in meditation, we process to our studios;
a choir of crickets chants orisons.
Ah, the contemplative life, floating through days
without schedules, appointments, car pools, the grace
of days to write in, time strung out like a rosary.

In a shining meadow of goldenrod, asters, grasses
gone to seed, a herd of cows appears, our bovine sisters,
robed in sleek habits; heavy molars click a slow cadence,
sweet green breath steams in the air. The grass
is always there, and it is always green.

Here, there is no morning paper, no nightly news,
no one knows what day it is, the date, only the season,
autumn, the woods just starting to flame. Nights grow
colder, we lie in our narrow cells, between chaste sheets.
We rise to work like prayer.

My Friend E-Mails That She'd Like to Quit Her Job, but She Doesn't Have Time

to resign. She writes, "Where has the fall fallen to?"
Corporate memos and annual reports pile up around her
like so many colored leaves.
The treadmill: work, commute, supper, errands,
skim the paper, scan the mail, fall into bed,
do it again tomorrow. Outside the window,
there's a maple tree that's green and gold, red and orange,
all at the same time. Every day the colors shift, intensify.
Today I walked the dog in the leaf-turned woods, the pine-
drenched air; even the light was golden. I picked
up two bags of drops for the neighborhood cider run
and ate one for lunch with a wedge of crumbly cheese.
The crisp snap, the juicy flesh, the rosy skin.
Then I waxed the kitchen cabinets until they glowed
like old honey, and I wrote a few lines.
I received no pay.
Here in poetry's lonely offices, no hope of promotion,
no IRAs. Around me, yellow sheets of paper cover the table,
spill onto the floor.

from
PARIS

sometimes y press, 2002

At the Cimitière de Montmartre

We came down the hill from Montmartre,
disappointed that it was full of Americans
from the Place du Tertre to Sacré Coeur,
and ended up at the lacy iron gates
of the cemetery, laid out like a small city,
long shady avenues, houses of marble and stone,
sunlight filtered through acacia trees.

We looked for the graves of the famous:
Berlioz, Truffaut, Émile Zola,
resting near the merely ordinary
in the dance of shadows and light. We sat
on a wrought iron bench, ate camembert,
pain de compagne, a kilo of cherries,
and, for a sweet moment, I loved you so completely,
when I die, I want our ashes to mingle; bury us in earth,
plant a rose bush, let it grow thorny, tangled,
and covered in blossoms; I want there to be no
separation between my skin and yours.

from
IMPRESSIONISM

*Winner of the Grayson Books Chapbook Award,
Grayson Books, 2004*

At the Atelier Cézanne

> *Pissarro taught him to paint without black. "Impossible, he cried at first; how can I paint relief?" Deprived of noir, he lost his power. But then he fell in love with color.*

And I, too, am in love with it, the patchwork of sunlight that falls
in intersecting lines and solid blocks through the great plane trees
of Aix, where we sit in the square, sipping dark coffee, listening
to the music of water in the fountains. Cézanne said,
the principal thing in painting is to find the distance,
but sometimes there is too much space between us, vast blue
stretches of the Gulf of Marseilles. In his paintings, even the sky
is broken in planes, blue rocks, chunks from the firmament's quarry.
Warm ochre. Deep green. Cold blue. Rosy apples in a white bowl.
The weight, the heft of them, repetition and refrain. He painted
the same mountain over and over, dragging canvas and easel
up Les Lauves day after day, where Sainte-Victoire still rises
in the distance, elusive, unreachable.

from
THE WHITE POEMS

Barnwood Press, 2001

for Judy Krol, 1951-1995

Prologue: Meditations on Grass

And now, it's beginning, the first shy tints of green
on the trees, a leafy scrim overhead,
and the grass, an improbable green for us who know
how soon it fades to the darker tones of moss and jade,
how it crisps in the August sun, bleaches
to dun, to bone. All flesh is grass.
And underneath this green air, cancer
spreads its rhizomes,
its tendrils sprouting in too many friends:
breast, skin, lung, bone, ovary, brain,
their green time running out.
The yellow wands of the willow sway over the creek,
tiny green buds beaded like tears.
Soon they will flesh out in elliptical leaves:
lancets, knives, blades. All grass is flesh.

Because the Body Is a Flower

Walking in Monet's gardens at Giverny,
with my husband of eighteen years, down a path
of pink tulips in a drift of forget-me-nots.
The whole garden, in fullest bloom:
poppies, peonies, lupines, a rainbow of irises.
The willows bend their green veils
over the water lily pool. We stop on the footbridge,
framed in wisteria: waterfalls singing with bees.
How we forget to love one another,
in the tangle of everyday life.
Let us lie down and love, here in the flowers;
kiss my skin, it is petals, the velvet falls of iris,
the heart of the peony, its voluptuous curves.
Let us become flowers, casual and gorgeous
in our brief hour, in this iris-scented air,
this light of cut glass and fine wine,
for already the petals are starting to fall;
they cover the ground in a dusting of snow.

1992: Faith

When my friend calls, long distance, early one Saturday morning,
I listen, knowing there's something wrong, think it's her
eighty-year-old mother, surely not her, she's younger than I am,
only forty. When she says, "I have breast cancer," there's a quiet
on the line, as I search for something to say. And then she
tells me it's spread to her spine, and there are no words for this.

And because there is nothing I can do, I go out to the garden,
dig the hard March ground, turn over ice crystals in the cold dark
soil, and plant peas, little gray pebbles, tuck them in with a slap
and a chink that might be a substitute for prayer.

For in spite of everything, June will come again, and those little
pairs of leaves will make their run for it, ladder up the air.
And these peas will fill their pods with sweet green praise.

October Light

where the air turns to honey, thickens, earth's ochre hour.
Here is the map of perfect weather, the brief sweet
return of sun before the short gray days at year's end.
Trees on the hills dance into fire: amber, scarlet, copper;
fields of corn blanch gold under the sky's bright glaze.
These are days you believe will go on forever, a blank
calendar stretching, endless, everything slowly turning to
gold. Sun pours through sycamore leaves, warms your bones.
Inside these ivory cages, we carry the seeds of our death,
like the black stars in the white heart of an apple.
Maybe it's in the ovary's dark purse, or buried
like a crocus corm in a soft hill of dirt. Sumacs flame
crimson, magenta. How can we believe these days will end,
that cold winds will blow, that snow will fall?

Meditation in Mid-October

Right now, just the tips of basil have been brushed
with frost's black kiss, but it's coming soon, that clear
still night when Orion rises over our house
and the dew falls in an icy net of stars.
On a small farm in Wisconsin, my friend's cancer spreads.
Piece by piece they've pruned her body.
Now they want to harvest her marrow.
They are promising her eternal life.
Soon, every blazing leaf will fall to earth,
stripping the trees to their black bones.
Soon, the only flowers will be the ice roses
wind etches on glass in diamonds and scrolls.
And if she refuses the surgeons
and their dazzling promises? The geese know
when it is time to go, head south.
We hear them pass overhead on starless nights,
wedges of bells in the cold thin air.

November, Sky Full of Bruises,

the way the light pulls away, night closes in early.
My friend is entering the hospital for six weeks
of isolation. They will pull the marrow from her bones,
let it leak out slowly the way this November light leaves,
then transplant it back to her body for the long wait,
for the white cells to grow from a few flakes to intermittent
flurries to a steady snowstorm, white and pure.
Alone, in a clean well-lit room, to cultivate the secret heart
of whiteness, to look ahead to a season called recovery.
But now she enters the long tunnel, burrows in for sleep.
November, and the light leaves early.
The woods are bare, trees stripped
to their bones. The earth is silent,
waiting for snow.

Total Eclipse of the Moon

Here we are at the end of the year, nearly the solstice,
a bad year, a close friend finding cancer in her breast
and back. Ten years ago, in the middle of the night, we had
an eclipse party, pulled sleeping children out of bed,
set them in lawn chairs to watch the moon disappear.
All the neighbors came, some bringing sugar donuts and black
coffee. Now this friend is fifteen hundred miles away in a white
hospital bed, while here in Pennsylvania, the last light
is slipping away in the west as the full moon rises,
earth's shadow eating at its lower half.
My friend has written her Christmas letter. The word "joy"
appears nine times. She is moving towards lightness,
the still white center of absolute zero.
As the shadow waxes, the moon turns from flat silver
disc to a third dimension, globe full of milk.
And the darkness steadily grows. Even though
this eclipse is predictable, included with the weather,
we hold our breath as inch by inch the light goes out.
Now it's a sliver, a thumbnail, a shred,
and then the last gasp of light is gone.
My husband and I hold each other hard, lean against
the empty swing set, stare off at the gap in space
where the stone in the sky used to shine.

1993: Hope

Winter sunlight, fool's gold, pours in the south window,
fails to warm. Weak as tea, pale as bone, insubstantial
as dust on a mantle, water falling over stone.
The ground outside hard, white as the hospital bed
where my friend waits after her marrow transplant,
hoping her white count will rise. I watch birds at the window—
sparrows, titmice, finches—the plain brown, the speckled,
the ordinary, no flashy travelers up from the tropics,
where winter is a verb, not a state of the heart.
I go out to fill the feeder, feel silky grain slip
through my fingers: millet, proso, corn. Little birds,
little angels, singing their small songs of consolation.
A thin drizzle of sun slips through clouds,
a strand of hope against the icy odds.

For a Friend Lying in Intensive Care Waiting for Her White Blood Cells to Rejuvenate After a Bone Marrow Transplant

The jonquils. They come back. They split the earth with
 their green swords, bearing cups of light.
The forsythia comes back, spraying its thin whips with
 blossom, one loud yellow shout.
The robins. They come back. They pull the sun on the
 silver thread of their song.
The irises come back. They dance in the soft air in silken
 gowns of midnight blue.
The lilacs come back. They trail their perfume like a scarf
 of violet chiffon.
And the leaves come back, on every tree and bush, millions
 and millions of small green hands applauding your return.

And Then, The Mastectomy

The cautious surgeon felt it was not necessary,
that chemotherapy had scoured the errant cells,
left her clean and white as new milk.
But he was wrong, they were buried deep,
like the shining seeds
in the heart of an apple.
Now they are taking her apart, piece by piece,
pruning her body, lopping off a breast like a rose in full
bloom, cream white, shell pink. They are ripping pages
from her book of years, soft summer nights, trees turning
into dark water, fireflies rising in the sweet grass.
And still the stubborn cells multiply and divide,
an evil arithmetic, the clock ticking away.

Breasts

Men would think of melons, hard white moons,
but women know breasts are soft,
a well-washed quilt with satin edging, a pillow of feathers,
a bowl filled with cream. For that's what we are, tenderness
and comfort. A warm bed on a black night. Sweet milk
for a new baby, rosebud fists in a cotton gown.
My friend's small lump has turned into nightmare.
How can she agree to let them slice that part of herself
as casually as slipping a knife in butter?

Losing a Breast

is not like a hot knife slicing through butter.
During minor surgery, I was awake when they cut my face,
and the flesh was reluctant to leave, tough to sever,
pulled and tugged like the moon at the sea.
Breasts are nothing hard like melons with their thin skins
and moony flesh, but soft, clouds piling up
in a summer sky, a field full of dreamy sheep.
And flesh clings to flesh, peaches to their stones,
mollusks to their shells, velvet and silk,
pink and white, full in the mouth like a ripe plum.
In the summer sky, a half-moon rises, brimming with loss.

Equinox

Another October. The maples have done their slick trick
of turning yellow almost overnight; summer's hazy skies
are cobalt blue. My friend has come in from the West,
where it's been a year of no mercy: chemotherapy, bone
marrow transplant, more chemotherapy, and her hair
came out in fistfuls, twice. Bald as a pumpkin.
And then, the surgeon's knife.
But she's come through it all, annealed by fire,
calm settled in her bones like the morning mist in valleys
and low places, and her hair's returned, glossy
as a horse chestnut kept in a shirt pocket.
Today a red fox ran down through the corn stubble;
he vanished like smoke. I want to praise things
that cannot last. The scarlet and orange leaves
are already gone, blown down by a cold rain,
crushed and trampled. They rise again in leaf meal
and wood smoke. The Great Blue Heron's returned to the pond,
settles in the reeds like a steady flame.
Geese cut a wedge out of the sky, drag the gray days
behind them like a skein of old wool.
I want to praise everything brief and finite.
Overhead, the Pleiades fall into place; Orion rises.
Great Horned Owls muffle the night with their calls;
night falls swiftly, tucking us in her black velvet robe,
the stitches showing through, all those little lights,
our little lives, rising and falling.

1994: Mercy

After years of mild Januaries, the hills and fields
buff and sand, like some rough slumbering animal,
winter returns; dozens of storms pile up snow shoulder high.
Night temperatures sink below the horizon of zero;
the thin pale sun, a cup of weak tea, fails to warm.
After last year's rounds of chemotherapy, bone
marrow transplant, more chemotherapy, my friend's cancer
has returned to her spine, turning her body's architecture
fragile. Lately I've been walking at night, stars
riddling the hard black sky, the way cancer is gnawing
her bones into lace. But she stiffens her back,
shoulders into chemo's biting gale.
You do what you have to do.
Soon, her hair will fall out again in clumps.
She looks out the window where her gardens lie under
the drifts, sees irises and peonies, green grass.
Another front moves in from the west; the snow keeps coming
down.

Dogwoods, Virginia

Along the spine of the Appalachians, spring is breaking out
in tentative green strokes in the understory, the glory
of dogwood and redbud, the return of the birds.
Before I came south, I spoke with my friend
in Wisconsin, our voices traveling faster than the weather.
What we take for granted, like walking. Or sitting erect.
Or days without pain. Or living to fifty. But now the cancer
has travelled up her spine. I imagine it as dogwood petals,
stiff and white, lightly veined in pink and green, rusty nail
holes hammered through each edge. Now the grass comes back,
a tender green. Purple violets, like tiny bruises,
mark the lawn. She said her veins are collapsing,
hard to get one open for chemotherapy's healing rain.
This winter, the snowiest on record, it seemed that spring
would never come, that the snow would keep on falling.
But everything turns, the dogwood petals that flutter and fall,
the tight new bud already forming. Along her spine, cancer
continues to open its terrible blossoms, almost as if a cloud
of butterflies had lightly settled on a hard brown bough.

In the Late Summer Garden

Green beans lose their adolescent slenderness,
broaden in plump pods. One pumpkin swells,
fills a corner with its orange lamp.
At night skunks slink in to dig for grubs;
in the morning we see their small excavations.
My friend's cancer has grown, spread to her femur
and liver. Everything that can be pruned has now been taken.
Tomatoes spark starry yellow blossoms, hope against hope.
Some will turn into hard green marbles, but the sun
has moved past equinox; days shorten and cool.
My son is learning his multiplication tables;
he flips flash cards at the maple table.
Numbers multiply like random cells. I am learning
the simpler but harder facts of subtraction.

After first frost has done its damage, I will rip out
the tangled vines, blackened marigolds, basil, cosmos
until nothing remains of the once green jungle.
I will turn over the soil, smell dark earth rise
like a river, work in compost and humus, believing
in the resurrection. Every year I feel my tap root sink in
deeper. My friend is learning how to let go,
to stop making plans.

Today she sits in the sun with a cup of coffee,
black and rich, stirs in sugar and cream.
There is no point in denying the body's hunger.
She spreads thick butter and honey on toast.
She would like time to stop now, the sky, blue as radium,
the hills, bolts of calico, red and yellow, gold and green.

Like a late maple leaf, burning in crimson,
she's hanging on with everything she's got.

She Tells the Dealer, Three More Cards

A thin sickle moon hangs in the western sky
over the house where my friend used to live.
Her blood count decreases as cancer deals
her another bad hand. Her backbone is turning
to ivory dust; her platelet counts diminish
in spite of transfusions. The sky is a vault
of black ice; the starry dust of the Milky Way
flung over our heads, Wisconsin to Pennsylvania.
She is buying new clothes for spring, a ring
of blue topaz to wear at night. She has backed
dark horses before, long shots going out at 100:1,
and won. She plays blackjack, shoots craps, gets comped
at Reno. Even though these odds are stacked
for the dealer, the house, she keeps on playing,
rolls the dice, rattles them bones.

1995: And She Never Gave Up,

not even at the end, when they started
measuring time in months, then weeks.
Winter was endless, sheets of snow
winding down from Canada, piled up
at the edge of the road like slag from the mills,
and so she flew down to Nassau
to feel the sun one more time, soft wind full
of flowers and red and blue birds, sugary sand,
water of liquid aquamarines. She hid
her black and blue legs under a flowered skirt,
perched a straw hat on her bald head.
Came back to find platelets low, red blood cells
gone, started over the rounds of transfusions
and treatments. Spoke hopefully of a new drug.

At her daughter's hurried-up wedding, the sand
running more quickly now, she wore gold lamé,
a curly auburn wig, pretended her jaundice was tan.
The grandchildren she wouldn't live to see flew off
to the future, nested high up in the coconut palms.

Requiem

It is early March, each day a little bit greener,
crocus and snowdrops already in bloom, daffodils
sending up the tips of their spears.
When summer comes, we will take you to the river,
trickle your ashes through our fingers.
You will return to us in rain and snow,
season after season, roses, daisies, asters,
chrysanthemums. Wait for us on the other side.
The maple trees let go their red-gold leaves in fall;
in spring, apple blossoms blow to the ground
in the slightest breeze, a dusting of snow.
Let our prayers lift you, small and fine as they are,
like the breath of a sleeping baby. There is never
enough time. It runs through our fingers like water
in a stream. How many springs are enough,
peepers calling in the swamps? How many firefly-spangled
summers? Your father is waiting on the river bank;
he has two fishing poles and is baiting your hook.
Cross over, fish are rising to the surface,
a great blue heron stalks in the cattails,
the morning mist is rising, and the sun is breaking
through. Go, and let our hearts be broken.
We will not forget you.

Letter to Judy

And now the lawn greens up by inches,
though the weather's changeable as a teenager
dressing for school. If I could call you,
I'd say that daffodils are blooming by the forsythia,
a thicket of sparks, that the world has turned green
and gold. Three years ago when we heard the diagnosis,
I knew what metastatic meant, that we would not grow old
together. The woods are still brown and bare, the Little
Jordan running cold and clear, and colt's foot, the first
flowers, rise up through the oak leaves, bright burning suns.
After you died, I wanted the seasons to halt dead in their
tracks, the stars to stop their whirling pinwheels.
Beside the house in the sweet woodruff, anemones
are opening, delicate shells of blue, pink, and white.
We planted them in my garden and yours when you still
lived here. They have spread, filled in all the bare spots,
I could tell you that my peas have already sprouted.
And now spring drags itself in, reluctantly, inevitably,
on the song of tiny peepers and white-throated sparrows.
Soon the long shadows of August will fall across the lawn,
and the neighbors will drink peach daiquiris on our porch,
a distillate of sun. And the rest of our lives will go on,
brightly colored balls of yarn, unwinding, without you.

UNCOLLECTED POEMS

1989-2005

The Year Winter Never Came,

the grass forgot to turn brown.
Birds hung around, canceled
their flights. Flowers bloomed
out of turn. The sky was a relentless
blue. Too much clarity, too much light.
What I missed most was the melancholy,
the low notes, the way that gray days full
of fog and clouds closed us in, shrinking
the boundaries, made me want to wrap up
in a wool afghan in front of the fire, listen
to the wind's thin violin playing in the chimney,
while snow's erasure covered the debris,
turned the lawn into a new sheet of paper,
before juncoes and finches stamped out messages,
printed cuneiforms in languages we'd forgotten,
made their marks on the untranslatable world.

Leaving the White In

To get true white in a watercolor,
you have to leave blank spaces, let the paper show
through, paint around it. Here, in the San Joachin valley,
the irrigated desert stretches into row after row
of orange trees, almonds, grapes, to where
the foothills of the Sierra sleep, tawny animals,
in the dusty golden haze. I'm visiting a friend
from college, twenty-five years rolling back,
and we've stopped for vanilla ice cream, sit in dusty mauve
booths that could have been painted by John Register,
whose picture *Waiting Room for the Beyond*
we talk about, all that cool glowing space. She tells me
why she's always tired, her white counts rising—

The heat is on us now, like a hard-breathing animal;
the light's of pale gold olive oil, iced tea.
She shows me recent paintings: El Capitain in Yosemite,
a stark white wall floating on a sky of cobalt blue;
she is glazing it over and over, working it up,
building the layers of paint to catch what the light
does to granite; in another, she's painted an old man and his dog,
the plaid of his shirt around his full beard, the folds
and creases in his worn denim overalls, the dog's soft fur.
The white isn't paint but paper; everything glows.

She steeps green tea in hot water for both of us,
here together, two old friends from Jersey,
drinking and talking by the sun-dappled pond.
She paints the light, the California light,
that dances off the Mantilija poppies, the desert flats.
She wants to paint the world, the entire edible world
full of pomegranates and eggplants, before her blood tires
of the virus in its sluice.

Now night falls abruptly, its inky wash covering the sky.
We do yoga, eat bowls of rice, drink more tea.
Jasmine fills the air; the moon floats up in its chalice of bone.

Shoveling at Night

The only time we could be together as a family was shoveling
at night with the snow still falling, so my father could get
to work on time the next day. The white birds of our breath
rose in the black air. Here, my brother's long silences
didn't matter, covered by the shovel's sharp grate. I could
lose myself in the rhythm of lift and fall without being called
idle or lazy. I bent my head to watch those white stars
fall out of the black sky, stuck out my tongue to taste
the flakes. I wished it would stop, that the yellow bus
would come, with its flashing lights, and take me to school
where I might get a gold star or a bluebird sticker, away
from home, where his anger simmered like a stockpot
on the back burner. Our noses ran and chapped, fingers
became numb despite their woolen gloves, and our toes
in rubber boots turned to ice. My mother wanted to let us
go in, heat milk for cocoa, skim the thin skin from the surface,
stir in marshmallow creme. Words flew; the snow kept its
silence. We went on shoveling in the dark.

Making Strufoli

(a traditional Italian sweet)

In the weeks before my father's death, I make strufoli for him,
not knowing he will enter the hospital Christmas Eve,
not knowing he will never leave that high and narrow bed.
There are piles of presents yet to be wrapped red or green,
stacks of glossy cards to write, my work abandoned until the new year,
and I'm at the counter, kneading dough, heating olive oil until it spits.
A small blue flame of resentment burns. I'm in the last half
of my life. The poems I haven't written are waiting
outside the snowy window. But I'm in the kitchen, rolling
dough into fat snakes, then thin pencils. With the sharpest
knife, I cut them into one inch bits—a slice for the prom dress
he refused to buy, the perfect one, in shell-pink satin;
a chop for the college education he didn't save for—*She's just
a girl, She'll get married, Who does she think she is?*—a stab
for the slap when I tried to learn Italian from his mother,
my grandmother, whose recipe this is. The small pieces hiss
in the bubbling grease. They change into balls of gold. I drain
them on layers of paper towels. I don't know I will never make
them again, never mix in the roasted almonds, pour warm honey
over the whole pile, sprinkle Hundreds of Thousands, those tiny
colored candies, over the top. I only know the way my shoulders
ache, the weariness as I do the great juggle—family, house, and
work—trying to keep all the balls in the air. And when his stubborn
breathing finally stops, when his heart gives out at last,
I only remember love as something simple and sweet,
a kiss of honey on the tongue. I take this strufoli that no one
else will eat and spread it on the snow for the starlings and the crows.

Worlds End

Wind-hush through the beeches and hemlocks,
wind-rush down the mountains, through the bare trees.
Water-music of the Loyalsock, green ice shelved
along its edges. We are chinked-up tight in a small log cabin,
roar of wood-breath in the cast-iron stove. At the pine table,
my husband peels an orange, and sweet citrus enters the room,
the sun coming out to play. No deer. No rabbits.
A cold that could nail bones. We are down
to what really matters, keeping warm, staying alive.
My son saws endless lengths of wood. We work
to keep the fire going, play Monopoly, Uno,
Chinese Checkers. Mugs of hot chocolate.
Sausage and cheese, sharp mustard. Wedges of apple.
Chunks of the forest go up in flame. Just before
bed, we walk single file down the hill to the washhouse,
our visible breath, scarf-lengths, trails out behind.
This is as dark as it gets on this planet,
as if the book of the night has just been written,
and we're standing here open-mouthed, reading the white-hot
star-spelled stories as if for the first time.

In January, My Middle Daughter Leaves Home

The seasons open and close like a fist,
and now it's winter, season of bones.
One blue jay at the feeder, flicker of a gas jet.
The millennial odometer turns 0 0 0.
There is no difference between horizon and hill,
white on white on white.
I listen to Verdi's *Requiem* driving down the turnpike,
the snow making its own white music,
and all the lines slant downward.
Crows clot the woods with night.

Snow Geese

Late winter, early spring—loss
followed loss, but still the snow
didn't fall—thousands of snow geese
have settled in the local cornfields
and abandoned quarries. They are exotic,
visitors from the arctic, pure white
except for the edges of their wings
tipped in black, and birdwatchers come
with their binoculars and scopes.

When they flock in the cornstalks and stubble,
the field is full of snow. When they rise,
a cloud lifts into the sky. Each one is immaculate,
bright as an angel, but that is too simple. And what
is their message? They lift off, an awkward flotilla,
nothing like the chevrons of their Canadian kin.
Week after week they linger, and we grow used
to their muffled calls, the blizzard of their wings.
The grass turns a little greener, forsythia spills
yellow on the banks. Then, abruptly as they came,
they're gone, and the lawn is full of emptiness.

Bright Star

> *...Rachel weeping for her children; she refused to be consoled, because they were no more.* —Matthew 2:18

Nothing in this day of green grass, flowering trees,
an eggshell-blue sky, speaks of grief, but it is there,
like a small creek running through the field
of the body. This is the season of expectation
and promise, when the death of a child seems even more
out of time. The cardinal sings its one sweet note,
cheer, cheer, but you hear it as weep, weep.
When petals spill from the apple tree, pink
and white, you think of graduation, weddings, all the things
that will not be. The bright blossom of the sun, after
months of gray skies, only makes you want to draw the blinds,
close the shutters. For how can the world break into blossom
and bird song when your heart is broken?
Winter was better.
We were supposed to be closed in.
Now green rises from the earth; everywhere there are shoots
and buds and tendrils, the same old new beginnings.
There is no consolation, only the sun, bright as a dandelion
in a child's tight fist.

Sadness Falls

We walked home between the houses, the dried grass,
the color of late winter, the gray sky,
the row of apple trees bent as old women.

How innocent we once were, before Sue moved,
before cancer took Judy down,
when our children played under these trees
with their dolls, petals drifting onto their hair.
They picked mulberries, made jam out
of five pounds of sugar and all the stems.

In winter, they lay down in snow, brushed wings
with their arms, poured maple syrup in bowls,
sold painted rocks door to door.

They were Indian Princesses, fathers and daughters,
pals forever. Red Feather. Bright Star.
Grew up into their beauty, went off to school.

Now one will not come home.

Away at college, on a Saturday night, too much beer,
dancing on a window ledge, one minute she was there,
one minute she was gone.

This is the house where grief has come,
unpacked his terrible suitcase. My friend, the mother,
chooses flowers, as if planning a wedding
that will not take place.

The father sits alone on the rusty swing.
The dried grass, wisps of blonde hair.
In the cold air, threads of geese braid and unwind.
We hear their cries long after they're gone from sight.

Sorrow Puts on Her Blue Dress

He has set me in dark places. —Lamentations 3:1

It's spring again, a sky of forget-me-not blue.
The light itself is a flower, the grass so sharp and new
you might cut yourself if you fell. And this is hell.
To go on living after the death of a child.
You have to get up each morning,
make coffee, pretend to go about your work.
Try to eat some cereal, get it past the lump,
as if you had swallowed an egg,
whole, like a black snake.
Now the earth reinvents itself, draws up
from the roots. Even plain brown twigs break
into blossoms of heliotrope and cream. Flashy tulips
spring from the dirt, yellow and red.
You see only their black hearts.
One day, you may learn how to love
the world again and all its breakable beauty.
But now, as the sun pours out, golden as honey,
your heart constricts to a fist of ice.
And it is always winter.

Nine Days in April

Virginia Center for the Creative Arts

I

In Vermeer's paintings, light is always falling
just like here, in sweet Virginia, where spring's
already come, lilacs and phlox, soft air
on bare arms, descending. Peepers are calling
from the trees; there are dogwoods, white
and pink, everywhere, as if a cloud
of butterflies has come to ground. Haloed
in hazy green, the woods are coming back to life.
At twilight, the scent of lilacs drifts
through the open screen, the sky turns lavender,
and this first day's work is put away.
Nothing but false starts today,
first lines begun that simply go nowhere;
filling yellow paper with my erratic script.

II

Filling yellow paper, my erratic script
wanders over the blue ridges and green fields
where cows munch green grass that yields
rich milk, like Vermeer's maid, whose hips,
wrapped in a thick blue apron, are rolling hills
themselves. The earthen jug, the crusty bread, the buttery
light glazes her face and arms, spills
onto the table and floor. The thing about memory's
that it's a thief, stealing what it should
preserve, the past, stop all the clocks.
I'm trying to remember what it felt like to be five,
first days of school, the smell of library paste, arriving
late, the stomach butterflied, new crayons in their box.
I'm trying to be good.

III

I'm trying to be good, write 500 words a day
even though outside the sun is streaming

like a thousand dandelions gleaming,
and the sky's the blue of washed chambray.
The purple prose of redbud trees is
scribbled and scrawled outside the lines.
Hidden in the grass, violets, buttercups shine,
but gosh, how hard this writing business
is—it's easy enough to just repeat a slick
lyric, a villanelle or two—
What challenge is there that I've not tried,
that also calls to something from inside,
blends head and heart as Vermeer drew
the light? A crown of sonnets just might do the trick.

IV

A crown of sonnets sure *would* do the trick,
could capture this experience—away
from home, nine days to see if I could pay
attention to myself for just a bit.
And so, today, I took a break and drove
to town, a thrift shop, bought a raw silk
blouse of Chinese blue, a tee shirt swirled in gilt
and glitter, earrings of gears and sequins that I love.
Came back, wrote for hours, went for a massage,
felt all the knots along my shoulder blades untie,
walked down the winding road, the mustard
blooming, thick as butter
spread on bread. All I
know is: a day like this is nothing but a blessing.

V

What a blessing it is, to be in this space,
no cleaning off the desk when the school bus comes.
The only sounds, the birds and bees that hum
and dither—which flower should we light on next?
In the woods, light falls, reflects off dogwoods,
rafts of phosphorescence,
illuminations, decrescendos
of lace. Each morning, I do yoga, get the blood

moving, then back inside to dig in memory's mine.
Each sonnet's getting harder now to write,
but the challenge has been thrown down like a glove
or crumpled petals littering the ground. I'd like to prove
that I can meet this task, and take delight
as one word, then another, falls in line.

VI

One word, and then another, falls in line
like geese wedging their way down the sky,
a vast scroll of paper yet unwritten. I
roll a sheet in the typewriter and begin,
again, to try and pin down what's elusive,
some insistent bird that whistles from a bush,
"Here, here, here I am," then vanishes
while I am left to struggle with the narrative.
Like *Girl Reading a Letter at an Open Window,*
I wish the light would flood in from the left,
paint me slickly gold, tell me what comes next.
But I am in the dark, no map, no text,
just following my heart as night falls soft,
covers us with her obsidian wing.

VII

Night covered us with her blueblack wing,
but now it is the morning, the last day—
here, the closest thing to paradise on earth. May
I be truly grateful for this stay, though squeezing
these last lines is getting tougher.
Last night, we had a concert, Brahms
and Currier on grand piano, wine on the lawn,
Caesar salad, grilled tuna, and strawberries for supper.
The lilt of southern vowels, drawling—
But this last sonnet's waiting to be woven,
threading the radiance of spring, memory's snapshots,
pictures at an exhibition, birdsong snippets,
into the poem's loom, the descant of love.
In Vermeer's paintings, light is always falling.

Rapture

Peepers, tiny tree frogs, punctuate the night,
their small song a promise of spring's return.
Overhead, the stars tap out their ancient stories,
and a comet appears, out of the darkest
reaches of space, from somewhere past Pluto.
The last time it came by, the Great Pyramids
were being built at Giza, Rome and Athens
were still centuries away, hunter-gatherers
roamed the Illinois Valley, and the Inuit
followed the rhythms of musk ox and caribou.

Now, in the new millennium,
we are bombarded daily with more information
than we can process, the endless
noise of television, more bad news
than the human heart can stand.

Standing here alone, under the blackboard
of night, away from any ambient light,
everything I know falls away,
and I'm back around the campfire, looking up at sparks
flying in the dark, seeing the comet every night
for weeks, its glowing heat, the luminous tail
thirty million miles long streaming and pulsing
like smoke from a single candle, a diaphanous scarf,
the breath of God. I am standing alone in this black night,
feet on the ground, mouth open, breathing in stars.

April Slips on Her Green Silk Dress,

a soft lilac shawl across her arms,
and dances to the small fine music of the rain.
I was away for a week, writing, happy to be alone
and working again, but then home began to tug
at me, the way the earth pulls the rain
down to meet it. And I love the road,
the journey, the whole difficult trip of it,
the long slow uphill climbs, the unexpected
bends, the side roads, the false starts,
every wrong turning. Dogwoods fill the woods
with their white light, kid gloves worn at a ball.
I'm going down the road, singing with the radio.
And my heart is as green as the rain.

Blue and White and Blue

Just outside my window, the Montmorency cherry
has thrown itself into full bloom, white
as a bride, yards and yards of lace. The sky
beyond, deeper than azure, an infinity of blue.
Last week, two children in Colorado shot
their classmates, tried to destroy the school.
Today the ripples reach Pennsylvania;
a bomb threat shuts the junior high.
Above us, the sky stretches so far.
Those children will not come home, even the killers.
All the empty beds. And a small war bumbles on
in the Balkans. Houses bombed to rubble.
Galaxies of stars bloom in the cadmium sky.
Bees hum their little songs.
On television, newspaper, radio,
the news of the world, this unbending sky,
this tree shedding shrapnel on the lawn.

August

Summer sings its long song, and all the notes are green.
But there's a click, somewhere in the middle
of the month, as we reach the turning point, the apex,
a Ferris wheel, cars tipping and tilting over the top,
and we see September up ahead, school and schedules
returning. And there's the first night you step outside
and hear the katydids arguing, six more weeks
to frost, and you know you can make it through to fall.
Dark now at eight, nights finally cooling off for sleep,
no more twisting in damp sheets, hearing mosquitoes'
thirsty whines. Lakes of chicory and Queen Anne's lace
mirror the sky's high cirrus. Evenings grow chilly,
time for old sweaters and sweatpants, lying in the hammock
squinting to read in the quick-coming dusk.
A few fireflies punctuate the night's black text,
and the moonlight is so thick, you could swim in it
until you reach the other side.

Retriever

If "Heaven is a lovely lake of beer," as St. Bridget wrote,
then dog heaven must be this tub of kibble, where you can push
your muzzle all day long without getting bloat or bellyache.
Where every toilet seat is raised, at the right level
for slurping, and fire hydrants and saplings tell you, "Here.
Relieve yourself on us." And the sun and moon
fall at your feet, celestial frisbees flinging themselves
in shining arcs for your soft mouth to retrieve. Rumi says,
"Personality is a small dog trying to get the soul to play,"
but you are a big dog, with an even larger heart, and you
have redeemed our better selves. Forgive us for the times
we walked away, wanted to do taxes or wash dishes
instead of playing fetch or tugger. In the green field
of heaven, there are no collars, no leashes, no delivery trucks
with bad brakes, and all the dogs run free. Barking is allowed,
and every pocket holds a treat. Sit. Stay. Good dog.

After September 11

If I say *God is good,*
you nod, because you also believe.
But if I say *MY God is the one true God,*
that's when the troubles start. So many wars
waged in the name of peace. *My missiles
are bigger than your missiles.* In the end,
when we are dust, will it matter who won?
One blue sky, fragile as a robin's egg,
covers us all. When we sleep, grass
is our last blanket. Maybe the stars
spell different stories to you, to me,
but in the darkness of the night,
they are light enough to see by.

Saying Good-Bye

> *Apparently trivial detail...can show us the world, the beauty to which we are always, sooner or later, saying good-bye.* —Robert Kelly

October, and the late afternoon sun slants in,
lays down a glaze of gold from the west.
It's time to cut basil, snip and strip
the dark green leaves with their breath
of anise for pesto on winter nights
when the sky is a lid of polished glass.

It's time to dry oregano, thyme, mint,
to simmer apples and cinnamon, mill them
down to sauce, a rosy reduction.

All summer, I've put up jars of jam:
raspberry, blueberry, blackberry, peach.
They sit smugly in the cellar
like money in the bank, their lids sealed
with such sweet certainty.

One night, a year from now, or twenty, or ten,
one side of this brass bed will be empty, one
pillow undented, one space under the log cabin
quilt smooth as stone. Sooner or later, one of us
will sleep alone. And all these nights, katydids
arguing their did-nots/did-toos outside the screen,
when sleep takes us before love does, will be long
and black and full of regret.

Apples Fireworks Guns Ammo Honey Jelly

sign on a roadside stand near Ruckersville, VA

Country of pulled pork, ham biscuits, red birds, collards
and cheese grits, of scuppernong jelly and muscadine wine,
drawled vowels that rest on the tongue sweet as this honeyed
light coming up over the hills, the soft sloping shoulders
of the Blue Ridge, split-rail fences, mistletoe topping
the highest trees. Land of kudzu, Osage oranges, bittersweet
vines, rifle shots off in the distance....

A low train whistle sounds, and the longing starts
in the deep pine forest of my heart, away from home,
family, my house with the wooden shutters. It pulls at me,
like a zipper up a cardigan, hearing the Interstate
where the semis growl and lumber, all four lanes
like a long run of good weather, calling me home.

/

All Souls' Day

Say November woods.
Say the colors of earth: ocher, sienna, umber,
a hearth where the fire's gone out.
Wind scours trees to their bones.
A chevron of geese cuts a wedge in the sky.
Imagine a hawk the color of winter.
On the day of the dead, he seeks a thermal
and soars. The dead rise, too,
will-o-the-wisps of mist and haze,
tobacco smoke from Indian pipes,
the plumes of tall grasses.
They are always with us,
tangible as breath,
fill the interstices of then and now.
In the November woods, cold air
settles like a blanket.
The sky tucks itself in.
Everywhere, the silence of all the folded wings.

Sewing

I'm looking back at the fifties, bathed in the yellow
light of nostalgia cast by the overhead fixture
in my mother's kitchen. I'm fifteen, the future
as unmarked as a bolt of fabric unrolling before me.
I thought it would scroll straight ahead,
like a seam running through the presser foot
of my old Singer. I could become anything.
But what I want now is to look like one of those girls
in *Seventeen,* an outfit for every occasion,
everything ironed, crisp and perfect.

Now I'm here, on the other side of fifty, looking back
at the girl who didn't know she couldn't have it all,
who thought she could do anything she started,
took apart her cheerleading jumper, reconstructed
it to a tight princess line. When the girl down
the street couldn't find a dress for the prom—
no store carried size ones and threes—
I took on the project, cut down a pattern, turned
three layers of ice-blue lace, silk organza,
and nylon netting into a dream of a dress
that is still dancing on the glossy yearbook page.

I thought I could alter the world, patch it back
together like my grandmother's quilts,
no project too difficult—
just lay out the pattern, make the first cut.

The Mothers

I

We gathered to give a baby shower
in absentia for the yet-to-be-born,
two-thousand-miles-away first grandson
of a friend whose youngest child died
binge drinking. Grief, the uninvited guest,
squeezed in, sat down on the sofa. But we oohed
and aahed at the tiny sweaters, booties, rattles, bonnets.
We know the end of the story,
but we love the beginning anyway.
We filled our china plates with shrimp,
broccoli quiche, cream puffs, lemon squares,
talked about our grown children
and the one who wasn't there.

II

Later, at the art museum,
two Vietnamese children from the family
sponsored by our church were chosen
for the Emerging Masters' Recital,
Paul on cello, Angela on violin.
I sat next to my friend Kathy,
and we remembered our work—
me teaching English as a Second Language,
she negotiating Social Services—and how if we knew
how hard it was going to be, we'd have never signed up.
But aren't we all refugees, searching for our lives,
and don't we all become orphans in the end?

III

And now I'm at the university, seeing
"The Vagina Monologues," where my red-
headed middle daughter is playing a black
homeless lesbian, and where I am so lost

in the power of the words, for a short while
I forget who she is, shining in her cherry taffeta
prom dress from Goodwill. At the end, the play shifts
from the sexual to the sacred, the opening between
two worlds, the way we all came in, part of the wheel,
the hoop, the great turning.

Acknowledgments

Grateful acknowledgment is made to the following publications in which these poems first appeared, some in slightly different versions.

A Song for Occupations (Wayland Press): "A Month of Sundays"
The Advocate: "Matchbox Cars"
America: "American Pastime," "Amusement Park"
The American Poetry Journal: "The Year Winter Never Came"
Anima: "Looking for the Comet Halley," "Rebekah Ziegler at the Quilting," "Persistence"
Appalachia: "Snow Geese"
Ascent: "Rose Multiflora"
Barnabe Mountain Review: "Requiem"
The Beloit Poetry Journal: "Field Guide to North American Birds"
Bless the Day (Kodansha America): "Auguries"
Borderlands: "My Friend E-Mails That She'd Like to Quit"
Caprice: "At the Atelier Cézanne," "And Then, the Mastectomy," "In the Late Summer Garden"
The Chiron Poetry Review: "Bright Star," "Sadness Falls"
The Christian Science Monitor: "Throw a Stone Into the Water, See the Ripples Spread"
The Comstock Review: "Dogwoods, Virginia," "Sorrow Puts on Her Blue Dress"
Confluence: "Shoveling at Night"
Connections: "The Rose Villanelle," "The Snow White Sestina"
The Denver Quarterly: "Grating Parmesan"
Deros: "Paper Money"
The Devil's Millhopper: "Patty's Charcoal Drive-in"
Electric Acorn (Ireland): "November, Sky Full of Bruises," "Breasts," "She Tells the Dealer, Three More Cards"
Everyday Blessings (Sourcebooks): "Diminuendo"
Four Quarters: "The Stone," "Writers' Colony"
Fringe: "Nine Days in April: VCCA"
Garden Blessings (Viva Editions): "January Thaw"
The Greenfield Review: "Summer Women"
The Hiram Poetry Review: "Raspberries"
Karamu: "Equinox"
The Loyalhanna Review: "Worlds End"
The MacGuffin: "Sewing"

The Madison Review: "Personal Best"
Mélange: "Apples Fireworks Guns Ammo"
Nebraska Territory: "Twenty-Fifth Reunion"
Negative Capability: "Obbligato"
Nightsun: "Leaving the White In"
Nimrod: "Blue and White and Blue," "The Mothers"
One Trick Pony: "Saying Good-Bye"
Painted Bride Quarterly: "Gardening in a Dry Year"
Pandora: "Total Eclipse of the Moon," "Making Strufoli"
Passager: "Mercy"
Passages North: "Ordinary Life"
The Paterson Literary Review: "The Last Woman in America to Wash Diapers," "Florida"
The Pennsylvania Review: "The Mother of a Handicapped Child"
Phoebe: "Doing Jigsaw Puzzles"
The Piedmont Literary Review: "Yes," "At the Cimitière de Montmartre," "April Slips on Her Green Silk Dress"
Plains Poetry Journal: "Southern Tier"
Poems for a Beach House (Salt Marsh Press): "Postcards from Hawaii"
Poet and Critic: "At the Château"
Poetry Life and Times: "Letter to Judy"
Poetry New Zealand: "Rapture"
The Poetry Review: "The Lost Children"
PoetryMagazine: "And She Never Gave Up"
Poets On: "Form & Void," "The Children of the Challenger League Enter Heaven," "Audubon Life List," "Learning to Speak Neurosurgery," "For a Friend Lying in Intensive Care"
Potato Eyes: "Visiting the Pumpkin Farm"
The Potomac Review: "August"
Proof Rock: "Christ Comes to Centralia"
Red Brick Review: "Meditation in Mid-October"
The Roanoke Review: "Hope"
Rock & Sling: "Retriever"
Small Pond: "Losing a Breast"
South Dakota Review: "The Refugees"
Valparaiso Poetry Review: "Driving Under the Clerestory of Leaves"
Welcome Home: "Burn Unit," "In January, My Middle Daughter Leaves Home"

West Branch: "Fever," "Tenth Anniversary," "Recipe for Grief," "Skating After School," "Looking for Loons," "Unclaimed Salvage & Freight," "The Wine Tasting," "Coming in from the Cold," "Meditation on Grass," "Because the Body Is a Flower," "All Souls' Day"
Windhover: "Faith," "After September 11"
Yarrow: "Echolalia and the Mockingbird," "The Shell Gatherers of Sanibel," "Winter Light," "October Light"

"After the Storm" has been set to music by Dale Trombore.

Special thanks to these editors: Harry Humes, Karl Patten, Ruth Daigon, and June Cotner, for their support of my work, and to the Virginia Center for the Creative Arts for the gift of space and solitude in which many of these poems were written.

Cover artwork, "Autumn Confetti," by Irene Miller (imillerphoto.com); author photo by Lincoln Fajardo; cover and interior book design by Diane Kistner (dkistner@futurecycle.org); Gentium Book Basic with Cronos Pro titling

About FutureCycle Press

FutureCycle Press is dedicated to publishing lasting English-language poetry books, chapbooks, and anthologies in both print-on-demand and digital (ebook) formats. Founded in 2007 by long-time independent editor/publishers and partners Diane Kistner and Robert S. King, the press incorporated as a nonprofit in 2012. A number of our editors are distinguished poets and writers in their own right, and we have been actively involved in the small press movement going back to the early seventies.

The FutureCycle Poetry Book Prize and honorarium is awarded annually for the best full-length volume of poetry we publish in a calendar year. Introduced in 2013, our Good Works projects are anthologies devoted to issues of universal significance, with all proceeds donated to a related worthy cause. Our Selected Poems series highlights contemporary poets with a substantial body of work to their credit; with this series we strive to resurrect work that has had limited distribution and is now out of print.

We are dedicated to giving all of the authors we publish the care their work deserves, making our catalog of titles the most diverse and distinguished it can be, and paying forward any earnings to fund more great books.

We've learned a few things about independent publishing over the years. We've also evolved a unique, resilient publishing model that allows us to focus mainly on vetting and preserving for posterity the most books of exceptional quality without becoming overwhelmed with bookkeeping and mailing, fundraising activities, or taxing editorial and production "bubbles." To find out more about what we are doing, come see us at www.futurecycle.org.

The FutureCycle Poetry Book Prize

All full-length volumes of poetry published by FutureCycle Press in a given calendar year are considered for the annual FutureCycle Poetry Book Prize. This allows us to consider each submission on its own merits, outside of the context of a contest. Too, the judges see the finished book, which will have benefitted from the beautiful book design and strong editorial gloss we are famous for.

The book ranked the best in judging is announced as the prize-winner in the subsequent year. There is no fixed monetary award; instead, the winning poet receives an honorarium of 20% of the total net royalties from all poetry books and chapbooks the press sold online in the year the winning book was published. The winner is also accorded the honor of being on the panel of judges for the next year's competition; all judges receive copies of all contending books to keep for their personal library.

Made in United States
Orlando, FL
01 November 2023